build a business from your kitchen table

For Laura
with love

Sophie Cornish

Holly Tucker

build a business from your kitchen table

Sophie Cornish and Holly Tucker
with Jessica Fellowes

SIMON &
SCHUSTER

London · New York · Sydney · Toronto · New Delhi

A CBS COMPANY

First published in Great Britain by Simon & Schuster UK Ltd, 2012
A CBS COMPANY

Simon & Schuster UK Ltd
1st Floor
222 Gray's Inn Road
London
WC1X 8HB

www.simonandschuster.co.uk

Simon & Schuster Australia, Sydney
Simon & Schuster India, New Delhi

A CIP catalogue record for this book is available from the British Library

ISBN: 978-1-47110-211-0

Designed by Kate Wright. Typeset by Nick Venables

Printed and bound in Italy by L.E.G.O SpA

CONTENTS

CONTENTS

For every one of our small business partners.
Your talent and commitment make this
your story, too.

LETTER TO THE READER

> 'Remember, Ginger Rogers did everything Fred Astaire did, but backwards and in high heels.'
>
> **Faith Whittlesey**

Dear Reader

If you've picked this book up and are wondering whether or not it's for you, let us help. Our proposal is simple. We want this book to be the bible for anyone who wants to start a business from their kitchen table. Perhaps you're a high-flying corporate exec who wants to escape the rat race, or a parent who wants more time at home with the children but still needs to bring in (at least) half the household income. You might be happy to sweat your 9–5 for a few more years but want to keep the creative spark in you burning bright, and plan for when you're ready to quit your regular salary. Or you might have big ambitions, right now, to start a business that's going to make you rich and famous. There may be two of you, looking forward to working together, or you could be planning on going it alone. At the very least, you've had a fantastic idea and need to know how to get started. If you're any of these people – this book is for you.

We know, because we did it ourselves – mistakes and all – and this is the book we wish we'd had when we started. Now we run a multimillion-pound company, have won numerous awards and have an actual boardroom of our own. But we started at the kitchen table only a few years ago.

Our business, notonthehighstreet.com, provides a website that is a single marketplace for thousands of independent sellers, most of whom are designer-makers, some are manufacturers and some are retailers. They create and sell their own collections of products, and fulfil all the orders they receive themselves. What we do is provide the technology, the business advice and the marketing for them to grow. Most work from home, some from a shed in the garden and some from studios or offices. Some enjoy being small and independent, others have built substantial businesses with several employees.

This means that our best advice doesn't only come from our story – it comes from several thousand stories, covering a broad spectrum of humanity. We've seen the common errors that beginners make when first translating an idea into a business and we've triple-tested these recipes for success. This book is full of real people: stories of highs and lows from those who have been there, done it and made the t-shirt. And we speak in normal, everyday language – that means no obtuse jargon, no trendy acronyms designed to confuse. (Any business words that do need explanation will be highlighted *like this* and can be found in the Jargon Buster at the back of the book. Website addresses for services suggested, and more, can be found in The Directory.)

Around 90 per cent of our sellers – we call them partners – are women, which does mean that while our business advice applies to anyone starting a new company, regardless of gender, many of the difficulties and conundrums, as well as positive inspirations, that might occur in the process are, for the most part, peculiar to our sex.

We're both mums, and that does affect the way we approach things and how we wrestle with finding time to fit in everything that fights for our attention – we've got a couple of chapters all about that, too. We understand what it is to want the best both for our families and our business. We're fiercely ambitious for our company. More than that, we want all our partners to be successful too.

Because of the nature of what we do, we know how it is to run a company that makes a small run of handmade products, as well as how it is to manage a multimillion-pound company that negotiates investment deals with venture capitalists and is growing on an international level. But for this book we are concentrating on the smaller end of the scale – we want to talk about how it is to get started and run your business from home, whether it's selling products or a service. Your idea might be to sell something you've designed and made, or it could be a consumer service – such as children's portraits, baby massage or party planning – or a B2B (business-to-business) service such as graphic design or PR. This book is for all of you.

But remember that even the biggest of companies had to start somewhere. So while we're concentrating on the first baby steps your business needs to take, we're catering for the ambitious, too. Throughout the book, we'll be pointing you towards growth and asking you to think about how to scale up your business. This isn't a guide for dummies: you need to be made of the right stuff, and we'll be asking questions throughout that are designed to test you and your ideas. We're taking you on a journey – this book is for you as you pause at the crossroads and wonder which direction to take.

So make no mistake – this is a business book. It ain't easy and we're not going to pretend that it is. As you read, we'll be prompting you to ask yourself if you've got what it takes. Working from the same table that your family expects to eat their supper off can be hard at times. And it will seem like a picnic when you're fending off your bank manager's calls for loan repayments.

When it comes to coping with the challenge of balancing our home and work lives, we think of it less as juggling, more as dropping balls all over the floor. We're not going to regale you with stories of how we got up at 5am to do yoga, before serving our children homemade muesli and floating into the office a few hours later. We're more likely to scrape

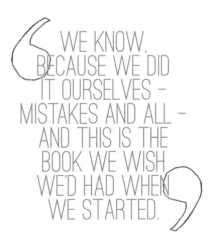

WE KNOW, BECAUSE WE DID IT OURSELVES – MISTAKES AND ALL – AND THIS IS THE BOOK WE WISH WE'D HAD WHEN WE STARTED.

ourselves out of bed at dawn to catch up on emails, eat a fluff-covered sweet that we've found in our coat pocket for breakfast and screech into the office for a long day of decisions, tribulations and well, yes, jubilations. Because we do enjoy it, too. If you work for yourself, you've got the best boss there is: a slave driver at times, not to mention unsympathetic when you're ill, but also one who understands you and allows you to strive hard for your dreams.

So, go for it. We'll be with you, every step of the way.

Holly Sophie

Holly Tucker and Sophie Cornish
Founders, notonthehighstreet.com

PS: A NOTE ABOUT THE TEXT

Although we are two very distinct people, easily told apart when in the same room, we have a tendency to talk as a single entity when talking about the business. So we've written this book in this way. Try to think of us less as an annoying married couple always talking on the other's behalf and more as a closely allied double act, which is how we think of ourselves.

#1

THE STORY OF US

HOW NOTONTHEHIGHSTREET.COM CAME TO BE

> 'You better think big and dream big, right from day one.'
>
> **Sheryl Sandberg**

In the beginning was the idea. Remember the mid-Noughties? Before the recession was the credit crunch, and before the credit crunch we were all sitting on a looping conveyor belt of consumer-led indulgence. Consumption was gluttonous. We were overladen with designer labels and overrun with cheap, mass-produced, instant fashion. Bling was the password for anyone wanting to get ahead, or at least, into the coolest nightclub, and all they needed was to flash their cash – talent, wit and intelligence fell by the kerbside in the celebrity lifestyle chase. Whether you bought your latest must-haves from Prada or Primark, you bought them all the same.

Yet, a slow undercurrent of change started to pull some people in another direction. An alternative culture of shopping started to grow – one that celebrated the local, the organic and the handmade, but was more about the hip, less about the hip replacement. Antiques that were collectables, second-hand that was vintage and one-offs that were artworks. The people who bought into this new ethos not only found that the words 'farmers' market' and 'flea market' were soon tripping off their tongue with ease, but that there was a cutting-edge way to compete with their peers. Rather than trying to outdo one another with a flashier car or a more designer handbag, it became about 'sourcing' items from hard-to-find places. Houses were beginning to look more like boutique art galleries, holidays were more about writing your travel *blog*. Taking a bottle of plonk and bunch of flowers to a dinner party began to seem too obvious, almost old-fashioned. Instead, people started to show up with a handmade Christmas tree decoration or box of artisan chocolates – all designed to show what stylish, original yet thoughtful people they were. What's more, the edges began to blur between those who found these quirky things to wear, give or style their houses with, and those who had started to design and make them. For the first time, the producer, retailer and customer were appearing in the same place, working on the same side.

There was just one problem. To find these quirky, handmade, clever and beautiful *objets* meant trawling the country to find random craft fairs, or weaving around a myriad of tiny boutiques scattered across the city – whether that city be Glasgow or London. Or hiring an interior designer or 'gift-sourcer', whose services cost more per hour than the things they were finding. You either had to be absurdly style-obsessed or have lots and lots of time on your hands.

Equally, the producers of these highly desirable things were frustrated. They knew people wanted to buy their stuff – all the style magazines said so – but it was hard to let anyone know where they were. They could build a website, but how would anyone find it? They could sell from home, but then they could hardly rely upon passing trade. For the most part, they had to sell to friends or to one or two local shops and hope that word of mouth would get them some more customers.

Until we came along.

But we need to go back a bit further, to explain how we – Holly Tucker and Sophie Cornish – came along at just the right point, with the right idea, to turn it into notonthehighstreet.com, the multimillion-pound award-winning business that it is today. We know we were lucky – we saw the opportunity and it was good timing. But we're not saying that made it come easily. (No, really, we're not. What comes a bit later is how turning it from an idea into a business meant we sweated blood, cried big fat sobs of tears and came within a whisker of having to give it all up, which would have left us with nothing but memories and a ton of debt. So sit tight.)

Going all the way back, we were two very different schoolgirls, in two very different times. But we do have something in common: we both had fundamentally happy, comfortable childhoods. We are ordinary, in that sense. It's not about rags to riches or hardships overcome. We're telling our story here because we believe entrepreneurship is for everyone that really wants it. We hope that what we tell you about us helps you to feel that you can do it too.

Just for this bit, we'll tell our stories individually and come back together later on, when we finally met and our history began . . .

SOPHIE'S STORY

Sophie

In 1965, The Beatles got their OBE, I was born and so began a childhood that was happy but fairly chaotic. I went to eight different schools, either because my parents moved house or were trying to find a school I actually liked. I thought the whole education thing was nonsense and schools the most miserable institutions, so I didn't always work very hard, although I did care intensely about English and I took extra maths lessons – I instinctively knew it mattered. But I certainly didn't see the point in going to university afterwards. Also, I have to admit that my slight obsession with order and tidiness was already raging when I was seventeen years old and, having seen my older sister's student flat, I didn't think I could handle three years of mess and unwashed dishes piled in the communal sink. So I went straight to work.

This move was also a logical one because, although I was brought up with a healthy disregard for domestic niceties – hence my teenage rebellion taking the form of a need for order, which has never gone away – there was an almost obsessive work ethic in our family. My mum is the journalist and bestselling novelist Penny Vincenzi, and she was of the generation of women that believed they could 'Have It All' – the children, the career, the happy home. Her peers tried to break free from the tyranny of running a house – in the words of their heroine, Shirley Conran: 'Life's too short to stuff a mushroom.' From my viewpoint as the child of a successful writer, her work was sacred – and thrilling. In the holidays, I used to go with her to the office at the iconic *Honey* magazine, where she was features editor, and spend all day in the enormous fashion cupboard, which was stuffed with incredible outfits and glam-rock boots, admittedly tidying it more than lusting over the clothes. To me, working was the most electrifying and liberating thing you could do. It didn't even look that hard – they spent all day chatting, for a start – and school was never really going to cut it by comparison. On the other hand, my father ran his own business – later he was an inventor, and he was always a brave risk-taker when it came to his professional life. I saw the hard work that went into that, and I found it equally compelling. As a little girl I didn't play princesses and dragons, I played offices. I would get the magazine *Girl About Town* and see what jobs there were, working out how much I could earn and when I could buy my first flat. I was ten years old then.

Immediately I was out of my school uniform, I heard about an opening at what is now Hearst Magazines, the publishing company. A friend of my mum's put a word in with the health and beauty editor for me, so I got an interview and then – to my excitement and terror, knowing that this break was luckier than most people's and I had even more to prove as a result – the job as editorial assistant for *Cosmopolitan*. At the time, in the mid-Eighties, *Cosmo* was a definitive magazine, spearheading a generation of independent women and placing as much emphasis on money, success and self-reliance as it did on sex, fashion and beauty.

Scary though it was at first, it was a formative experience that defines me still. Here were forty or so clever and talented women at the absolute top of their game. Many of them were names that are well known now, going on to become 'first women' of their generation: first editors of Fleet Street, first to be directors of fashion and beauty houses, first to top the fiction bestsellers lists. Deirdre McSharry was the editor who was driving the UK *Cosmopolitan* brand under the direction of the legendary Helen Gurley Brown (the one who started the whole 'Having It All' notion in the first place), and she completely engendered the ethos of mentoring and supporting women to achieve their own success and independence. Far from being bitchy – which, by the way, I have never found an all-female environment to be – it was nurturing and educational.

Someone, somewhere was always making sure that all the juniors (me included) were learning and developing, and the culture there meant that there was never any doubt that if I wanted to go all the way, so long as I worked hard enough, I could do it. I got my first byline when I was nineteen years old, and many more followed. Standards were high, everyone took enormous pride in being professional, and the place was alive with energy and commitment to producing the best work possible. I learned to write to be interesting, instead of writing to get an essay grade. And I picked up a never-to-be-lost respect for immaculate text, grammar and punctuation. It was a unique place at a unique time. Everyone looked stylish and gorgeous, all the time. What's more, I got to spend days and weeks with some of the best photographers, stylists, models, make-up artists, art directors and graphic designers in the business. It gave me a rock-solid groundwork: when it comes to producing beautiful work, I know what's what.

I climbed up the ladder to the dizzy heights of beauty writer before moving across to *Good Housekeeping* magazine as the health and beauty editor. That was less alarming; I felt less afraid of making mistakes, and my knowledge and much-needed confidence grew a great deal under the kindness and talent of senior editor Sandra Lane, who herself went on to become one of London's best interiors photographers. But although I loved the writing and the journalism and the photographic styling, it was the consumer elements I really thrived on, such as compiling the shopping pages and discovering new brands. I was already witnessing in my colleagues that competitive edge which drove people to discover, wear or simply own new things that were completely different from anything that had gone before – even if they found them somewhere very ordinary, such as the local charity shop. (Now it's called 'sourcing vintage fashion'.) It created a challenge that I found more stimulating than publishing. Although many of the luminaries I'd worked with went on to do great things, I couldn't help feeling that with their brains, ambition and talent more of them could have built whole empires.

But that's a comment on the time as much as anything. Back then, in the Eighties and Nineties, successful women worked in the media. I don't know that I had even heard the word 'entrepreneur' then and it's not something I'd have thought to apply to myself, but I definitely had a business itch that needed scratching. At just twenty years old, I'd got a mortgage and bought my first property (as I'd planned to, when I was ten) and felt I was moving up in the world. Now, as a journalist, I loved the power to incite interest in a reader simply by highlighting a new product or small business. I do remember thinking that it would be an electric opportunity if you could make it possible for the reader to be able to buy a product the moment they saw it, instead of having to read the credits and then go down to the shops. This was long before the internet and *e-commerce*, but it goes to show how ready we all were for it, way before it happened. But whatever one called it then, I was getting interested in the propositions, ethics and motivation of consumers, products, business and retail.

When the opportunity came along to work on creative brand development for Boots No7 and 17 cosmetics, developing seasonal colours and new products, I leapt at it. For one, what could be more fun for a 24-year-old than to spend all day dreaming up new make-up colours, cosmetic formulas, packaging and product names and, for two, getting involved with the business side of the industry meant I could scratch that itch. My boss there, Barbara Attenborough, was herself an

THERE WAS NEVER ANY DOUBT THAT IF I WANTED TO GO ALL THE WAY, SO LONG AS I WORKED HARD ENOUGH, I COULD DO IT.

Sophie

entrepreneur and another exemplary example of a successful woman who was generous, kind and savvy. Through her, I realised that owning your success was what gave you the freedom to make your own choices in life.

Perhaps in recognition of this, in my mid-twenties, I decided to take a year out to live and work in Sydney, as well as taking a full trip around the globe. Maybe I had wanted to be a student after all. I got a new buzz while I was away – finding cool stuff from all over the world and packing it home. At any rate, I got that free-spirited existence out of my system, and came back ready to launch myself more definitively in the business world. I went to work in advertising, which was a natural move given the two areas I'd worked in to date. First, I joined an incredibly of-the-moment creative hotshop, GGK London, who were winning more awards than they knew what to do with. We were constantly celebrating and being celebrated. I loved working there.

But I was ambitious, and my best opportunities were more likely to be found in a big agency with big beauty accounts. I moved on to Publicis, where I managed campaigns for numerous clients, including L'Oreal brands, George at Asda and Monsoon fragrances. I brought everything I'd learned to that job and had thought this was the place that it would all come together, but it never quite fulfilled me in the way I'd hoped. We had a lot of fun, and there were a lot of very bright, ambitious people around, but it felt large and institutional, and it was my first real experience of the power of corporate politics. More than ever, I longed to do my own thing. Behind the scenes, I was working on a novel that I was convinced was going to make me famous – an advertising thriller – and, shaped by the magazine women of my formative years, believed that this was going to give me my big break.

The best thing about working at Publicis was that I met Holly, who came to work with me (by then a director) as a young exec. She was instantly and obviously exceptional. In so many ways she was like the people I'd worked with in magazines: energetic, creative, dynamic, confident. Goodness, she was confident. We got on extremely well from the off, and I became very fond of her as I witnessed her rapid climb through the ranks.

In spite of my gripes about that time, it was a happy one. Not only did I meet Holly there, but it was also during my advertising years that I met Simon, who later happily became my husband. Meeting him was a major turning point, for all the obvious reasons but also for others less so. Despite what you might assume of a City broker – and a man at that – Simon turned out to be on what we have come to call 'the quest' for the perfect item. I had always been driven by it, but falling in love with him turned it into something of a life's work for both of us. We spent most of our courtship in The Conran Shop and flea markets, finding vintage and retro things for our house, and it's always been Simon who has cooked incredible, stylish suppers for dinner parties with our friends. Exploring that world with him was very exciting.

Soon after Holly had joined the team at Publicis, I became pregnant with Ollie, my first, and despite my best attempts to keep it secret for a while at least, she was the one who guessed (very intuitive, as ever) and asked me outright. You couldn't mind: Holly was charming. But what I didn't know then was that this remarkably driven young woman would shape my future. When I left the company, in 1999, we kept in touch with coffee or lunch every year or so. I felt very maternal towards Holly and always anxious to know that she was doing OK, and life did get tough for her – but we went our separate ways.

With the age gap – there's eleven years between us – our social circles were different and having a second child inevitably meant I was getting more domesticated (though not very, in retrospect). With two tiny children at home, Honor and Ollie (now thirteen and fifteen years old), I wanted an alternative to the fifty-hour working weeks I was used to. For the most part, I took on consultancy and freelance work, writing for magazines about style and shopping, which gave me an insight into what customers were searching for. I was also commissioned to write a book about weddings (it was easy to do, as I was getting married) and joined a dot-com start-up, which gave me an early start in the e-commerce arena. Coming up to my late thirties, I'd finally figured out how expensive life was. It was time to start making my own money, calling the shots, shaping my own destiny, and grabbing life with both hands. All the time, I was searching for the right thing to do – I still needed to scratch that itch.

I was making progress. I set up a small business styling private and corporate events with my friend Nicki Marsh (now working with us on *social media*), which led to a course in floristry. I loved the direction that industry was going in then, with cool designer florists springing up, and rather fancied being able to create those impressive displays myself, not just order them in for my clients. I started making huge, gorgeous door wreaths one Christmas, and selling them at shopping fairs, which taught me two things: firstly, that making money out of flowers is difficult, flowers being perishable, expensive, fluctuating massively in price and a nightmare to store (I considered buying an old butcher's shop at one point, for the giant fridge), not to mention the routine 3am starts; and secondly, that selling through shopping fairs is one hell of a tough way to make a living. And I only did it for about two months.

But I had found a gap in the market. At that time, if you wanted to deliver flowers to, say, your stylish mother-in-law in Cornwall, you only had the option of standard bouquets from Interflora or one of the supermarket chains. If you wanted something funkier, the top florists would only deliver locally or, if it was outside central London, for crazy prices. I started to work up a business plan and got as far as finding a supply line. But I soon realised that I would either need premises to hold the large consignments from Amsterdam, which was expensive and risky, or I would have to join up with an existing flower contractor, in which case the *profit margins* would be very small. Still, I was up for it. I was ready for a big challenge.

My fate turned suddenly when, in the space of one week in 2005, just as I had decided to take the leap and move up a gear with the floristry, I finally got a top agent for the novel I'd been working on for years, I realised it was now or never with a third baby, and I got an email from Holly, almost out of the blue, asking if I might be interested in going into business with her . . .

HOLLY'S STORY

Punk rockers the Sex Pistols released *Never Mind the Bollocks* in 1977 and I was born the same year. A coincidence? Yes, of course. But I like the connection, though it's more about the plain-speaking than the pierced eyebrows. When I was six years old, my mum used to give me pocket money

Holly

in return for helping out around the house and it wasn't long before I was asking not only for more jobs, but better-paid ones.

Perhaps it's in the genes – my dad worked for Apple Records with The Beatles, my mum worked for Janet Street-Porter, and her French mother was an entrepreneur. Both grandfathers were self-driven and successful, too. We moved to Holland when I was seven years old and I went to international schools in Amsterdam and Antwerp; my best friends were Brazilian, Irish and Japanese. I learned to speak German, French, Dutch and English. Early on I saw that everyone does things differently and it's meant I'm always open to new ideas.

We came back to Chiswick, London, when I was fourteen years old and it wasn't long before I was holding down a job cleaning a pub, where I would rinse in Dettol the coins I found on the floor, so as to earn an extra quid or two. At fifteen, I was doing shifts every weekend as a silver service waitress and running the school tuck shop. I was always creative, too, and took up a quarter of the school's art room for two years with a huge sculpture inspired by Henry Moore. If I could do something, I always did it as big as possible!

In the summer of 1993, I took a work experience job at Publicis, the advertising agency, because I was already hungry for a career. I ended up working there for my entire summer holidays three years in a row, with a long commute each way, every day. I was excited to be doing it, but it crossed my mind more than once that my friends were enjoying long, hazy summers of delight instead. Still, I stuck to it and on the day that I was due to collect my A level results, Rick Bendel, then the chief executive of Publicis (now the chief marketing officer for Walmart's international businesses, including Asda), offered me a job as a junior account executive. I was eighteen years old. My mum and my sister had dropped me off at the interview and were waiting round the corner in our Peugeot 205. I got in the car, screaming with excitement about the job, and then we drove to my school to get my results. Design Technology, A; Art, B; Business Studies, E. Talk about ironic.

Job offer in hand, I dropped my plans to do an art degree and went to work. It was hard. I was young, I had to prove myself; I could always be found working hours as long as anyone there, yet I was paid the least: £12,000 a year. Out of that came my train fare, my rent, and – as a junior – most of the department's personal expenses too, which wouldn't be paid back for a month or two. One month, having taken the hit rather more than I should have, I couldn't pay my rent (I had left home after school, to move to a tiny flat in Harlesden, west London). Sophie was the account director on my team, and was so appalled by how little I was paid that she lent me the money. To

IF I COULD DO SOMETHING I ALWAYS DID IT BIG.

Holly

my absolute horror, I had to accept because I had no other option. I never forgot that kindness.

By the time I was twenty-one, I was an account manager and had a lot of responsibility, managing international clients and overseeing millions of pounds in budgets. I knew how to act as if I was thirty-five years old. But I wanted to move on: that same year, I bought my first property and married the boy I'd been with since I was fourteen. I went to work for Condé Nast, publisher of *Vogue* and *Tatler*, as a fashion ad sales manager for *Brides* magazine. From there I was asked to join a start-up online wedding site, Cool White. It was a great idea, showcasing cool, high-end bridal boutiques and services, but the world – and technology – wasn't yet ready for it.

Then, when I was twenty-three, I put on a lot of weight very quickly and couldn't understand why. Tests revealed that I had a brain tumour. That news alone was earth-shattering, but then I was told that, because of where it was, they couldn't operate. After more hospital appointments and tests, which were very distressing for my whole family, we discovered that it wasn't malignant and for the next five years, every three months, we watched it not grow. It's still there, but the doctors are no longer concerned as the chance of it growing now is extremely small. Nevertheless, at the time, the stress of discovering the tumour was huge and my marriage was also severely on the rocks. I was mature, but I just wasn't old enough to handle my world crashing around me. I knew I had to keep paying the mortgage but my health issues spiralled and, in all, I put on three-and-a-half stone in less than five months. The bridal website came to an end and, in order to keep working, I began freelancing as a consultant, troubleshooting for ad sales teams on magazines.

Two years later I still hadn't had a holiday because I was so booked up. But working that hard and going through a messy divorce was extremely tough. At that point, my angel from above, Frank, came along. I'd known Frank for most of my life – he'd even been at my wedding. He worked for the Metropolitan Police, was seventeen years my senior, and he gave me the courage and support I needed to believe in myself again. He moved in one month later and helped me battle to save my flat from being sold as part of the divorce. It was quick, but somehow we knew immediately that we were meant to be together.

It was while consulting for *The London Magazine* that I dug out my now trusty purple notebook, in which I jotted down all the business ideas I had. And then I had my light bulb moment.

With my illness in remission, I wanted to be creative again, and designed Christmas wreaths made out of unusual things then, such as chillies, oranges and cinnamon sticks. (I had no idea then that, by some strange kind of serendipity, Sophie was going through the same learning curve at almost the same time.) I planned to sell them at craft fairs and assumed there must be one in Chiswick, where I lived. There wasn't; so I set one up – Your Local Fair. My dad lent me £5,000 to get started. I finally repaid him last year.

Holly and her tiger helper

We had the first fair at Chiswick in 2003 and it buzzed. Many of the people who helped me then are working now for notonthehighstreet.com. Not least my dad, who is our *CFO*, my mum, who is a talent scout for new business, and my sister, Carrie, who is head of merchandising. Everyone there was supportive of me, but they were also glad to see the old Holly back in the game.

For two years I ran Your Local Fairs all over London, fitting it around the consultant ad sales work at *The London Magazine*. Doing both in tandem meant I could hire colleagues to help me with the website design and the marketing on a freelance basis. When your business is small, it's handy being able to do a deal over a glass of wine with your colleagues. It also meant that I didn't shirk the responsibilities of my core contract with the magazine. If anything, I was even more motivated. I would never take a lunch break, but instead would set myself a target of hitting £10,000 in *revenues*. Once I had reached that goal I would say, 'Now I can spend half an hour on Your Local Fair.' At the end of the year, the sales team I managed there won the company's top award.

But while running the fairs was exciting, it was a very up and down business; running events that relied on the weather meant the financials were always unpredictable, although overall we managed to break even. Happily, I got pregnant in the summer of 2004. Frank and I moved into our new home in the November of that year, I did my final fair on 16 December and Harry was born on 28 January 2005. The magazine contract came to an end and there was no maternity leave for me as I was self-employed, so when Harry was ten weeks old I had to get back to work. I started freelancing for my old client again, selling advertising. My sister Carrie came and worked as a nanny for me for free; she had

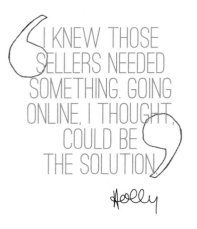

I KNEW THOSE SELLERS NEEDED SOMETHING. GOING ONLINE, I THOUGHT, COULD BE THE SOLUTION

Holly

just finished doing a degree in psychology with ergonomics and was helping me while using my computer – and my experience – to help her send out her CV. I kept saying to her, 'I just can't get this idea – of giving small businesses a platform – out of my mind.' I had discovered so many of them with fantastic products to sell. Fairs themselves, I now knew, were not the answer, but I knew those sellers needed something. Going online, I thought, could be the solution.

For four months, I split my time between selling advertising, running Your Local Fair and looking after my baby. I'd push Harry down the hall in his baby walker and he would slowly, very slowly, work his way back to me – by that time, I'd have managed to close a deal over the phone. Then I'd push him back again.

While thinking about how to take the germ of my idea online, I knew one thing for certain: I couldn't do it by myself. I had to find the right partner, who would provide strengths where I was weak. I went through all the people I knew and it was almost weird the way I kept coming back to Sophie. It was years since we had worked together and we had only occasionally kept in touch. I knew she was getting her own business off the ground, was sure her life would have moved on and that she couldn't possibly be interested. But Carrie kept pestering me: 'Have you emailed Sophie yet?' Eventually, I wrote to her.

I just knew she would be the right person – not only because of the kindness she had shown me in the past, but because I needed her yin to my yang. I'm very driven, but I'm not so hot on detail. Sophie had maturity, I already knew she could be impressive in meetings, she could stand up to people and she has an incredibly precise mind. But I didn't think she would be remotely interested.

Within twenty-four hours Sophie had written back.

She was interested.

Sophie: 'When Holly first told me her idea, I felt a cold trickle running down my back, like a dropped penny, and I knew immediately that this was something I needed to do. All the work that I had been doing on the magazines and in writing the wedding book – which was full of independent businesses that did one-off, beautiful pieces for a bride – told me that people wanted unusual, hard-to-find and original things for their homes, wardrobes and to give as presents. Even trying to find a way to deliver funky floral arrangements instead of relying on the bog-standard carnations was part of the movement I could see happening, where aspirational people wanted to demonstrate individuality and style. I also knew that those designer-makers were out there, but that they were almost impossible to track down. I knew, in short, that there was an appetite and now here was Holly with the supply.'

TOGETHER AT LAST

Within a day or so we had met up and begun work. From the start, we worked in each other's houses – off the kitchen tables – and we worked long hours. Sometimes, Carrie would cook us a stir-fry for supper, carrying it in with one hand, baby Harry in the other.

Holly: 'We worked from a funny little room in the back of my new house – we called it the 'B&B' because it had revolting Forties tiles on the walls. We took over the whole room, covering the walls with pictures of the kinds of products we were talking about and postcards from the small businesses that sold them, and sat at the table – the same one that is now my desk at our Richmond HQ.'

How the business developed was a lesson in the evolution of a start-up. When we first got together, we had the kernel of an idea to 'do something online', but originally we were playing around with the concept of a directory of businesses, not e-commerce.

Sophie: 'I first mooted the idea of actually taking money – selling stuff on the website. One shopping basket, lots of people selling. I tentatively suggested it, but Holly leapt at it.'

As we discussed the possibilities, we started to realise even more what it was that we were each bringing to the (kitchen) table. Because it is our dynamic, as much as anything, that makes this business work.

Sophie: 'Holly has big plans, talks a lot and is a real presence in a room of people. A true leader.'

Holly: 'Sophie might appear to be the quiet one, when she's next to me. But she's at her best producing her own work, collaborating in a small team, getting things done, and done right. So we would discuss the vision and the business model together – I would be the one who took an idea and ran with it to its furthest reaches, and Sophie would put together the first of many business plans. Writing one meant doing the heavy-duty research, understanding the market, the customer, the realities of getting a website built and launched, and thrashing out the detail – Sophie's work. I'm the one who builds up to an ambitious *financial forecast* that spells thrilling success. I am also the negotiator, signing partners up, sealing deals. Both of us are equally definitive of the business. Together, there is a balance.'

Sophie: 'We also naturally represent the two perspectives of the business. I speak and think for the shopping customer first: what's going to turn them on, what matters to them, what's going to make them notice us and, importantly, what's going to make them reject us. Holly knows the small businesses intimately, is thinking about what's right for them commercially, helping them grow, picking the products they should push to help them to success. Which isn't to say that we can't swap hats, and we do.'

Holly: 'Sophie brought twenty years of experience to our business, which included her work for magazines – researching things carefully, writing, proofing, presenting ideas, working with photographers and stylists – and some formal training in ad agencies. Sophie also has two sisters who are lawyers, which has influenced greatly the way in which she approaches things. All of these things together meant that if we did something impulsive or inventive, there was a structure, form and protocol there, too. As a pair, we have extremely high standards and began the business with an unbudging refusal to be anything but completely slick and professional from the first day.'

Sophie: 'At the other swing of the pendulum, Holly's drive was momentous, but as she was young she had not yet been through the ranks of any company to complete a training of conventional and best practice techniques. Holly invented everything she did from scratch, which meant she was unfettered by convention and had – still has – little truck with anyone who said something couldn't be done.'

This carefully weighted balance has also had one considerable bonus in that we rarely clash. We don't row, although that's not to say we don't disagree. When we do, it tends to be either a hearty and quick discussion, or a few hours of tension, and then we resolve it. On the whole, we both know that the one will bring a point of view that the other needs to listen to, and we're good at talking – or waiting – things out.

We did, however, carefully and deliberately consider how we would ensure that we could work together as business partners, even though we knew we were already good friends and colleagues. The key here was a long and detailed questionnaire, which we both filled out, and then each read the other's answers. In it, we had to be completely frank about our visions for the business, the time that we could give to it and our attitudes. We refer to it still. We would highly recommend any new business partnership to put itself through the same paces. (See Chapter 3 for the kind of questions we asked.)

That year, 2005, we went out and started to persuade our first partners to join us – more than that, to pay to join us despite the fact we were barely even a business yet. (Every seller – or partner – pays a one-off joining fee and a percentage of the checkout price made on the item they sell through us.) But we had at our fingertips the research we had already carried out, and this gave us confidence when we went to talk to them.

From the point of view of knowing our market, we were in a position of some strength because Holly had spent two years on Your Local Fair. We already knew that the sellers were out there and that they needed us. We also knew that there was a genuine gap in the market – we had no competition. We knew, in other words, that if we built it, they would come.

We had proof of this from very early on, long before we had anything we could remotely call a business.

Sophie: 'Months before we launched, I was at a fair, gathering *leads*, talking to customers and generally getting more research and insight. On this particular day, Holly had stayed back to call potential partners and effectively see if it would sell. It was a tense day and I was waiting to hear how Holly had got on, but dared not call her. Perhaps it was just too early, I thought, maybe too soon to ask or maybe just one will say yes. But eventually Holly rang, shrieking, 'They all said yes!' That was a vivid, never-to-be-forgotten moment. On the phone to her, I thought, yes, we are on to something.'

But before we could lay a single brick to build our business, we had to raise our first funds of £70,000 each, through begging, borrowing and raiding our savings. Even writing it down like that makes it sound a whole lot easier than it was. We are not the kind of people to have money knocking around – even now. It wasn't a case of 'Poor me, I have to dip into my savings', we really were starting from absolute scratch.

Holly: 'Frank even gave me some compensation money he'd been awarded for damage to his hearing. It took him six years to fight for and win that money, and he handed it over to me, almost without me asking for it. That was just amazing.'

Although we were, technically, putting our houses on the line (we could only just about meet mortgage payments at that time, so any kind of squeeze felt like a huge risk) and therefore the security of our families, it somehow didn't feel like that. We were completely confident and very excited. There is something unusual about us, in that we don't seem to feel the fear in the same way as others do. We don't know if it's our upbringings or just who we are, or simply the fact that we totally and utterly believe in notonthehighstreet.com. But the truth of the matter is, no matter how scary things have got – and sometimes that's very scary indeed – we've always believed that it will come right in the end.

If there was a spare coin down the back of the sofa, it went in the pot. We didn't pay ourselves a penny as most of that money went on building the site. But although we were passionate about our idea, not everyone was. Trying to raise the money for it was always one of the most stressful things, even when it went well.

Holly: 'Sophie called a few banks – the ones who promise that their life's purpose is to get small businesses off the ground – and only one seemed worth a meeting. She sent off our immaculate business plan and, to our excitement, a meeting and then a small loan almost magically materialised. It all seemed rather easy at this stage. Only later did we realise that – even when we were turning over millions – they would never be prepared to give us any more unless we handed over our houses as security. We managed not to bow to that pressure, but only just. If we had one piece of advice, it would be never to use your house as a guarantee for your business, no matter what the banks say.'

It's at this point we were given pertinent advice that has stuck: when you start a business, it's not about how commercial and savvy you are – it's how much pain you can take. Back then, we didn't really know what it meant. When we ran out of money a year later, we really did.

It might sound irrational, but if anyone rejected our business plan, we couldn't help but take it personally – whether they were sellers we wanted to work with or *investors* we'd pitch to. We'd write their names down and put them in box called 'You'll Be Sorry'. But there was an upside because even tiny crumbs of rejection can propel you towards success, or perhaps just away from failure. We became almost absurdly driven by our need for the business to win.

Less than a year after we had agreed to work together, in January 2006, we moved into our first office, Aaron House in Richmond, chosen for being the best halfway point between our two houses. It certainly wasn't chosen for its beautiful architectural properties. We had one room, then we negotiated a second with a

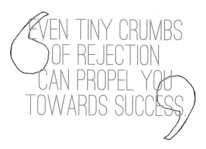

EVEN TINY CRUMBS OF REJECTION CAN PROPEL YOU TOWARDS SUCCESS.

connecting door. On the first day, four of us sat at our desks – us, Carrie and Louise Cullen (a friend of Carrie's, who was keen, sharp and available) – and for those first few minutes, we just looked at each other. It's not a moment we'd trade . . . but nor is it one we'd like to repeat.

Sophie: 'We had our one and only argument at that point. Holly went out and bought seven computers, although there were only four of us in the office. I was not impressed. That money had killed us to pull together. While Holly was going for world domination from the start, my eye was on survival to the end of the year. But of course, we soon needed those extra computers; as on so many other occasions, I later saw that Holly had been acting on her exceptional foresight.'

Looking back at photographs of that first L-shaped office, we recall the distinctly urban view (a grey tower block and the low, corrugated iron roofs of the industrial buildings next door), the weak warmth from the rapidly failing radiators, the harsh overhead lighting and the painted breeze blocks that made up one wall.

Holly: 'By Sophie's desk were pinned several print outs of various lists (super-urgent lists, priority lists, sub-lists, lists of lists) and a small black and white photograph of Ollie and Honor. By my desk were two large whiteboards with business-like headings such as 'Pending' and 'Band A', with scribbled graphs and pie charts. And of course my desk had a vanity mirror, with my make-up bag on standby. You could always find a sprig of cheerful flowers and a few small pots with a lilac orchid, bought by me on a crazed four-trolleys-full spree around Ikea in a hurried attempt to beautify our surroundings. Those orchids weren't even real, but such was the pace that Sophie didn't realise and watered them for months.'

Talk about not stopping to smell the roses. We did our best, but they were not pretty offices. Not that we cared too much. They were ours. We were running a real, live business and we felt so lucky to be coming into work every day in a company that was our own.

From the start, the team was completely connected. An old school friend of Holly's, Lucy Wood, came to work with us, and then her friend Summerly Devito joined a few months later (both are integral parts of our DNA). Our technical director, Joe Simms, was Louise's friend from university – he popped in one day to help us set up a programme to resize some images, and stayed with us for five years. Sophie's sister Claudia Vincenzi was our unofficial legal eagle, and Sophie's friend Julie Turner from *Cosmopolitan* days was now a *PR* expert who joined the team as a freelance consultant; several more people – including Lucy's sister Emma Wood, still very much part of our team – were roped in when we needed the extra help. Only four of us were on the (nominal) payroll, but as launch day loomed closer the truth dawned as to how much work was needed and it wasn't unusual to have up to sixteen people sitting on the floor with laptops, all of whom needed to be paid. We would look at them, working all hours, mentally multiply the hourly rate by the number of heads, and try not to faint at the total sum.

We learnt something important from this time. As terrifying and heart-stoppingly awful as relentless drive like ours can be – and under that pressure, we had no choice anyway, preventing us from eating or sleeping properly and taking us away from friends and family – it's when you feel comfortable that you should be really scared. Because it is the single moment you are complacent that your world is about to come crumbling down. We know, because this happened to us not once, but twice.

With all the excitement mounting about going live with our business and turning all our exhaustive, and exhausting, hard work into a tangible reality, we failed to see what was really happening.

Two weeks after we moved in to our office we had built a microsite to act as a showcase to promote the business while we were building contacts and selling membership. Insanely and masochistically, we created a countdown clock that announced our forthcoming launch as 3 April 2006, just two months away. It seemed such a fun idea at first. But it quickly tormented and terrorised us, as we found ourselves tied to the time-bound promise we had made to press and also to our sellers, who had by now parted with their cash. We had brought upon ourselves a sickening pressure to meet a deadline that was rapidly becoming unfeasible.

It wasn't until one week before the launch date that we began to realise that the agency we had contracted to build our main site had promised us the impossible. Of course we knew deep down that it wasn't viable for our site to be up and ready in time, but we allowed ourselves to believe their reassuring platitudes. We had almost one hundred paid-up sellers ready to go. We had told everyone we knew. All the journalists had been primed. We couldn't fail, we couldn't not do it.

The night before the launch date, it hit us. We were doomed. The site wasn't going to be transactional. The brutal truth was that we were about to launch a shopping website on which no one could buy anything.

So we spun it. We called it a 'preview' and invited all the visitors to the site that day to return later. There were 16,000 visits on our first day, which in any other circumstances would have been deemed a huge success. We could only hope they liked the look of what they saw enough to try us again. Our plan worked. On our homepage, we invited people to register on the site in a competition to win money to spend with us another day. When the emails started to come in, it looked like a computer meltdown scene from a Hollywood movie. They flooded through. Our little 'info@notonthehighstreet.com' email inbox was scrolling over and over for hours and hours, filling with thousands of email notifications that customers had registered with us. It's an experience we'll never forget.

In the end, the site had to be relaunched not once, but twice in the first year alone. The first, a week later, was to make it transactional, but that day did not go smoothly either. The basic fact was that we had made a mistake with the agency we had chosen to do the work: they were not up to the task, despite the full round of screening, checks and references. Joe, by then our technical director, had come into our lives at just the right time and now rebuilt the whole site from scratch – under wraps. We had to do that because if the agency knew, they'd also know we weren't planning on paying them their final invoice (which was already very overdue), and we thought they might be inclined to take the site down or block our access to the servers. This absolutely could not happen, so it became a terrifying secret mission, with our hearts in our mouths day and night.

At last, just as it became apparent that the original agency was twigging that something was really up, we made the switch. The first site had taken five months to build, the second took two weeks. The pressure was so intense, it was like some sort of prehistoric geological event – it forms you and redefines your whole being. Looking back on our emails from the early days, which are, after all, only six years ago, it's like reading our teenage diaries. We were so young and green. We've had to grow up a lot.

It's important to remember, too, that our business is not just about us, Holly and Sophie. It's about our sellers, our partners. We call them partners because we believe we are working with them, not for them or them for us. They give notonthehighstreet.com meaning. We feel deeply that there is a purpose to what we do, building and supporting small businesses, and presenting them to our customers with pride and confidence. We want our partners to be supported and communicated with at every stage, to let them know we're working with them for the right reasons and to share with them the opportunity, planning and decision-making.

But all of that brings with it a huge responsibility. We know that we affect people's lives and their livelihoods. Our company supports real people with real skills. We enable them to grow their business, and enable our customers to support them and make responsible buying choices in turn. It's the reason we get up in the morning: it drives us on and we absolutely believe in it. We know many of our partners as well as we know our own friends, and we want them to succeed. We're not saints, but we know it matters, and who else will champion this kind of business if we don't?

The winners of the 2011 Make Awards, our inaugural event celebrating the creative enterprise of our small business partners

Failure is not an option.

You'll find out in the rest of the book how it went after we finally got up and running. Yes, there's more hard work and some tough times – but some great ones, too. We wouldn't still be doing it if we didn't love it, which is why we want to encourage you to do it too. Because encouragement is what we're all about. We'll be putting you through your paces, but if you believe in your idea, then you must hold on. We wish we'd known back then that we were right to be so crazy in love with our idea and that we weren't experiencing the delusions of a mother who believes her child is the most beautiful one in the room. We did know, even when faced with cynicism or disaster, that this was worth holding out for. We knew that we just had to fight to get us past a point of trouble – because it was only ever a point, like stepping in quicksand. But if we'd known how successful we'd be, it would have been a whole lot nicer and a whole lot less traumatic. We're not complaining – we know we're playing the world's smallest violin. Now we have a team of over 100 people in our offices, with several thousand partners doing well, and have pulled in almost £100 million in turnover to date.

Guess who's feeling sorry for themselves now? That's right. All the people in the 'You'll Be Sorry' box.

WE ASKED OUR PARTNERS...

What has notonthehighstreet.com helped you learn about running your own business?

Jo Hargrave, Big Little House, retro home accessories: 'What hasn't it taught me is more the question. I have always said that the price of joining notonthehighstreet.com doesn't just cover the opportunity to sell, it comes with great business guidance as well. It sets a high standard which we can all transfer into our own business, like calendar dates for getting products ready, such as Mother's Day, and also key trends to look for.'

?

Sherrie Mead, the letteroom, alphabet gifts: 'It has shown us that we need to be much more forward-thinking in product development and seasonal changes, i.e. with photography and themes, and the importance of keeping ahead of trends and not resting on our laurels. It has also helped flag up possible disasters with licensing and legalities that we would have been unaware of.'

?

Claudette Worters, murano glass jewellery: 'I think it has taught me that business is constantly moving and changing – especially internet-based shopping – and you have to go with the changes to keep up. Customers will always want more from you, whether new designs, faster service or the personal touch. I have also learned to keep a tighter

Here I am at eighteen years old, in my first suit and working in my first job at Publicis. I'd not quite made the full transition to career woman yet, though – my mum still had to drive me to the train station to get to work.

Holly

This is me at twenty-eight years old, around the time I met Simon, and also Holly. The picture was taken for a pitch document (it did the trick – we won the job!). It might have been the Nineties, but I still had shoulder pads and a *Dynasty* hairdo.

Sophie

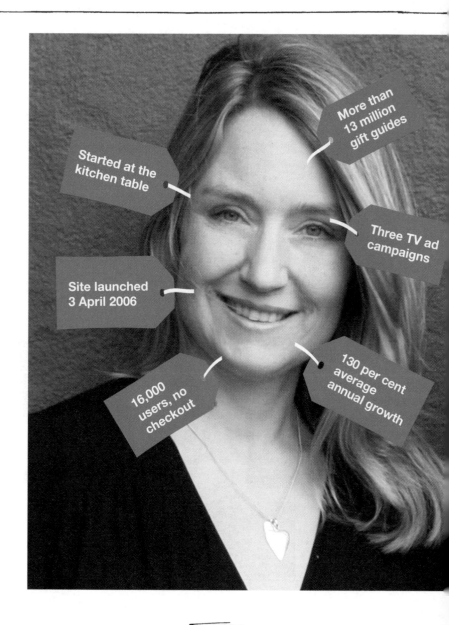

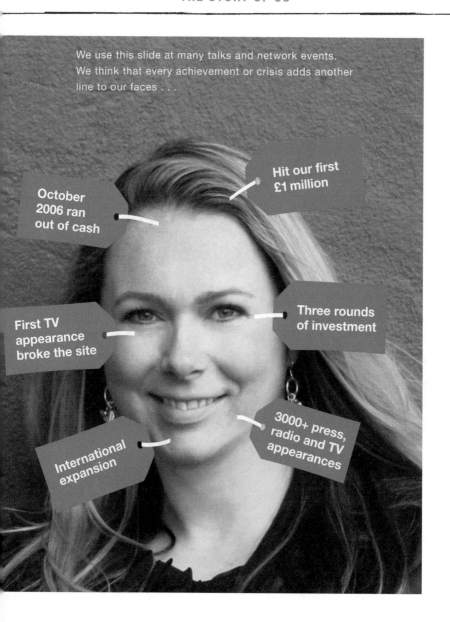

The two of us in our office now. We still do our best work sitting around a table together.

check on stock control. And although I am still nervous about the whole PR aspect of promoting my business, I feel that I do now have a better understanding of what is required, and understand I need to find more time for it.'

?

Gina Axell, Rosiebull Designs, embroidered textiles:
'Everything! I knew very little when I started, other than how to make my own products. It has taught me about sales figures, developing the right products and working with current trends, how best to photograph my products, customer service skills – the list goes on!'

#2

GETTING DOWN AND DIRTY

FINDING OUT IF YOUR IDEA
MEANS BUSINESS

'Genius is 1 per cent inspiration,
and 99 per cent perspiration.'

Thomas Edison

If you've picked up this book, it's probably because you've got a great idea for a business. Well, congratulations. Ker-ching! And all that.

But how do you know it's the right idea? What if someone else has had the idea already? How do you tell anyone about your great idea without someone else pinching it and doing it first? Have you had the whole idea, or is it just halfway to being a great idea? Supposing it is a great idea, but you're not the right person to turn it into a business. How do you even know if it could be a business? In other words, you're only 1 per cent of the way there. That's not to say it isn't a very vital and necessary 1 per cent. Think of it as the 1 per cent of DNA that makes the difference between you being you and you being a chimpanzee.

It's rare that a successful business idea is perfectly formed when it is first thought of.

Holly: 'When I had my light bulb moment of pulling together designer-makers, it took three years, an incarnation as a whole other business and Sophie coming on board to redefine it before it emerged as notonthehighstreet.com.'

For us, we had the key initial concept – to create a single platform for many independent sellers – that was the seed which flourished into the tree we have today. Equally, we had both had many other ideas in the past, seedlings that failed to thrive and died.

Holly: 'On at least three separate occasions, I had such a good idea that I had business cards printed up before I'd so much as found my first customer, let alone sold anything to them.'

Which reminds us: no printing business cards before you have made any sales. In fact, no business cards until you have made one hundred sales.

Sophie: 'I had also had quite a few ideas for a business. I even made one succeed for a while (styling private and corporate events). But perhaps it was my experience in the wider world of work that told me that Holly's idea was the one that had the magic spark. Together we had the right knowledge that helped us find the right *route to market* with the idea.'

There's nothing wrong with trusting your instinct. In fact, we rely on it all the time.

WHAT AN IDEA IS

Lots of people ask how to get an idea – but we all have ideas all the time. The question to ask is: which ones do I allow to take flight and which ones do I censor? Amazing ideas very rarely come out of the ether to take one by surprise. The best ideas are rooted in something tangible: usually it's the answer to something you want but can't find, whether that's an actual object or the solution to a problem. Nor does it have to be completely new: it will most likely be similar to something that exists, but a tweak – whether in design, supply, execution, price or location – makes it something better. You could be the first to pick up on a growing trend, and work out that there's a relevant product or service to be offered. If you're stuck for an idea, think about your own life and conundrums. Could you design, invent, create or provide the thing you want that you can't see anywhere else? We can't have your idea for you – we suspect you already have a few mulling over, and that's why you're reading this book – but we can tell you what to do with it once you've got one.

But just because something sounds fantastic, or gets you excited, doesn't mean it is fantastic. Feel the instinct – and then get practical.

Once you've mulled over your idea for a while, perhaps even talked it out with someone close to you and decided that it has got legs, then you're halfway there. But what you need to do next is something that will really pull it apart and test all the component parts, to see if it still works when you put it back together.

THIS TEST HOLDS THE KEY AS TO WHETHER YOUR BUSINESS CAN REALLY FLY.

We'd like you to do something that is not quick or easy, but it holds the key as to whether your business can really fly. If you can't find it in yourself to have a go at the following exercise, then you should seriously question whether you have it in you to start and run a business at all. On the other hand, if you relish this task, then you've got it. You're made of the right stuff. Don't be nervous – anyone can do it, so long as they want it enough.

What you write here will not be your business plan, but it will help enormously when you do come to drawing one up. It will sort the wheat from the chaff – the two-a-penny, common or garden ideas we all come up with from the stuff that successful businesses are made of. Getting through our acid test is a landmark in itself. Once you have completed the exercise, you will have something tangible and useful, something that gives you the right language and the confidence to talk to potential investors, supporters and customers. It will also give you the tools to answer back to the naysayers.

It's the notonthehighstreet.com 'Down and Dirty Test'.

Write the answers to all the questions we've set out below. Do this exercise as if someone else will read it. You need to fit your answers to each test within one or two sides of A4 paper. If an idea is good, it will sing off the page.

A word of encouragement: we know this seems like quite a task, when all you want to know is, 'Is this a good idea or not?' But think of this as an insurance measure. Tackle these questions now, and you'll find out things that will save you a lot of money and heartache further down the line. You'll need to do research to answer many of these questions – there's guidance on how to do that throughout. And if you can't get all the answers, or all the right answers, that doesn't necessarily mean you have to give up – it could just mean that you have to give a bit more thought in order to succeed. Because when we did these tests, that's exactly what happened to us.

1. THE ORIGINALITY TEST

This element of the test will help you not only identify why your idea is original, but why its originality matters. Your answers here will articulate whether customers are going to be excited by it, whether it has the necessary X factor and also if you have any legal constraints.

- Is this product/service unique? That is, can I be sure that my idea is not already done by someone else? If it is, have I put my unique stamp on it? What is my *USP* (unique selling proposition) that will compel customers to buy it?

- Is there a market for my product/service? If so, where and how big is that market? (Here you need to do careful and extensive research. But summarise it. Remember this document is meant to be handy, short and informative. See more below on how to do market research.)

- How will I deliver that product/service to the customer?

- Is there competition for the kind of retail space – whether shop, website, studio or consulting room – I'd need?

- Do I have any copyright/trademark issues with any other suppliers of the same or similar products/services?

- Can my product be ripped off easily? Or might it be unique only until someone finds a way to copy it and sell it for less? In which case, how can I protect my idea?

- Are there any regulatory issues that I have to overcome first? For example, health and safety, trading standards, etc.

2. THE COMPETITIVE TEST

It is possible to enter into a crowded market and do well – but it can be expensive, difficult and is not usually best done by a one-man business. This test will help you decide whether the marketplace is one that you can successfully compete in.

- Why will the customer want my product? Again, what is the USP?

- Can I price my product/service competitively, once I've considered the cost to produce it?
- Am I competing on price, or quality, or sheer uniqueness – or all three?
- Who is my competition and are they successful? (Even if your product is completely unique, the customer has alternatives, or is spending that part of her budget another way.)

For some quick answers here, you can easily check whether there's anyone out there who already does what you're thinking of doing. You can Google it, of course, or go to Companies House (where you will hopefully be registering your own company name before long). Any *limited company* must legally be registered here, and you can use their free WebCheck service to search for information on more than two million companies already in existence. The British Library Business & IP Centre is a great resource, too.

In addition to finding out company details, you can use WebCheck to view a company's filing history and purchase copies of document images and a selection of company reports. You can also choose to monitor a company and receive email alerts of any new documents filed at Companies House.

The results from all this research will also help you to crystallise in your mind just who will benefit from your idea. From there, you can optimise your marketing strategy (of which, more later).

3. THE FINANCIAL TEST

To be a business, it has to make money. We're never going to let anyone think otherwise, which is why we only call something a 'business idea' if it can prove it's going to be profitable. This is probably your most important measure of whether an idea is a good one. (You can do a fairly rough estimate here. For calculating costs down to the last red cent, see Chapter 6. You'll also see here and in several places further on that we assume you have an accountant or good financial advice – that's because you need it and we'll explain more about that in the Money chapter, too.)

- Does it make money?
- Does it make enough money to match the investment and time involved?
- Does it make enough money to allow me to give up the day job eventually?
- What sort of return on my sales should I make? (You should be making more than you would get if you left the money in the bank. Much more.)
- What sort of margins do other businesses make in the sector I am selling in? How do I compare?
- Have I got the cash resources to fund any losses? (Many start-ups lose money in the first couple of years, as it takes time to build up their business.)
- Have I worked out the direct cost of each of the products/services I am going to offer, including the cost of *raw materials* and labour?

- Have I considered which suppliers I will use? (Small businesses find it hard to get credit until they have an established business – you may have to pay upfront for supplies.)

TO BE A BUSINESS, IT HAS TO MAKE MONEY.

- What will my *overhead costs* be?
- What will be my wholesale or retail selling price to cover my direct costs and my overheads, and make a profit?
- Have I projected what cash is going to come in?
- How will I fund my initial investment to start the business up?
- Do I have access to sufficient start-up money to buy or manufacture stock to allow me to start trading?
- Where can I go for further loans or investment if needed?
- Have I talked to an accountant and asked for advice?
- Am I being realistic? Can I manage if things go more slowly at first than perhaps anticipated (as they almost certainly will)?

Holly: 'Those same ideas that I got the business cards for all failed on the finance test. I did the numbers and, luckily for me, my father was then an accountant. I spent a great deal of time looking at the idea through numbers and was forced to be realistic. All three businesses folded before even getting to the business plan stage. I was lucky I was able to move on and the rest is history.'

4. THE EXPANSION TEST

This final test will enable you to understand and map out the longer-term potential of the business. This is important – a business can only survive or have a future if it can grow. Then – and this is another critical reason for doing the test – you need to wrap that vision up and put it away for a while. It's good to know it's there, but you don't want it to distract you or take your eye off the more immediate task. Expansion can be made to sound exciting and easy. But the worst mistake can be to diversify too much, too quickly.

Planning ahead matters.

You also need to think about how expansion will affect your personal life and your family. Working seven days a week may bring in extra money, but at what personal cost to you?

- If my *core offering* – whether it's a product or service – took off, what would be next in store (whether a new product, line or brand expansion) and what would that mean to the business financially and in terms of *scaling up*?
- How would I cope with high growth?
- To what level do I want my business to grow? Am I ready to become the next Philip Green or Deborah Meaden, or do I only want this to be a part-time business giving me some additional income?

- How will I make sure as I expand that I plan ahead to cope with increasing demand: more staff, office space, warehouse facilities? (Many businesses fail because they're unable to cope with demand. They can't cope because they haven't looked forward or put aside enough cash to invest for future demand. The customers you fail then don't come back.)

There, you're done. We know it will feel like hard work just to get to the end of this exercise, but it's this document that is going to carry you through the tricky times in the future. We can't emphasise enough how important it is that you answer these questions thoroughly.

A brief word on...

THE IDEAS THAT FAIL THE D&D TEST

At the end of the Down and Dirty Test, there are three possible outcomes. Best of all – hurrah! – your idea passes with flying colours. What are you waiting for? Off you go.

Alternatively, our test will kill it dead. Don't be downhearted about that. Since starting notonthehighstreet.com, we've had lots of new ideas and lots of them haven't made it beyond this stage. Frankly, it can come as a relief when the test gives you a clear 'no'. You can put it to rest and concentrate on coming up with a new, better idea – one that is going to be much easier to execute.

But there's a middle ground. The good idea that doesn't quite stack up . . . yet. Your gut won't let it go away, but there's a lot wrong with it. That was the case with the early incarnation of notonthehighstreet.com, and it taught us one of the first laws of business: success isn't about having it easy, it's about how good you are at dealing with problems and obstacles. If it feels really right, don't be afraid to keep going back to that idea. Chip away at the hard questions and see if there isn't another solution. Is the competition really such a problem? Do you need retail space or could you do it online? Perhaps the technology you need is hard to build, but are you sure you're asking the right people to answer that question for you?

Holly: 'Try to find someone who runs a business that is about three years old – the point at which you should be over the worst but still a way from the finish line – and has had to overcome their own obstacles. It might just help to have a fresh pair of eyes. They could say that one word or ask that one vital question that is the key to seeing the way through to the next stage. I should add that you need to ask them very nicely – they won't have much time to spare.'

If you still can't reach a satisfying conclusion, then you need to 'let go with love'. It's a phrase we use a lot – it comes from Alcoholics Anonymous, appropriately enough, as ideas and business can be addictive. And with that, we'll leave you to make up your own mind about your idea.

RESEARCHING YOUR MARKET

Once you've passed the Down and Dirty Test, you can then get down to the nitty-gritty of finding out exactly where your market is. Working out who your customer is and what they want is critical and is a process that never stops. When we started notonthehighstreet.com, we had one advantage in that we had Holly's experience of two years with Your Local Fair. This told us that the designer-makers were out there, that they desperately needed marketing and business support, and we also knew that there were customers who wanted to buy from them. But would both parties be happy to sell and purchase online? Even just six years ago, online shopping was a relatively youthful and untried thing. People didn't generally have total trust that their credit card details wouldn't get stolen and there were news stories about online fraud and identity theft frequently in the newspapers. While Amazon and eBay were already successful, they were not yet enjoying the huge numbers of customers and usage that they do today. More than that, we were dealing with a genre of product that hadn't yet been sold online. When they challenged us, investors called these 'touch-and-feel' product types – things that people need to see up close and fall in love with. They weren't buying these things out of need, as with groceries, nor were they certain of the product itself, as with CDs or books. The only precedent we had was Natalie Massenet, who had proved that criticism completely wrong with high-end designer fashion at Net-A-Porter (a purely online venture). Would charming hand-painted signs, handmade ceramics, personalised jewellery and embroidered baby blankets break the mould in the same way?

To do our market research and answer these questions, we had to get out from the warmth of our makeshift office. We stood outside tube stations with our clipboards, trying to look as professional as possible, asking strangers to fill out our questionnaires. We canvassed potential customers by standing outside craft fairs and Christmas shopping events. On our first day, we stood outside the train station by Olympia, a huge exhibition hall in London. For some reason, we were convinced that we were going to get arrested for illegal researching or some other well-recognised crime. Then we plucked up the courage to go into the station, mainly because it was raining, but also because people were avoiding us and we thought we might have more luck if they couldn't go anywhere on account of their having to wait for their trains. In the end, we got on the train itself and pinned them down there. This is called *primary research* and means that you are talking directly to your potential customers.

Thankfully, not every bit of market research involves getting cold, wet and embarrassed. There are some brilliant online tools for research that will poll respondents, enabling you not only to identify your prospective customers, but to find out what they think about your idea. You can, for example, create multiple-choice questions (start with five) to ask the price people are willing to pay for your product or what they're currently buying/doing instead. Invite people to respond using online software that gathers responses and makes analysing your answers easy, such as SurveyMonkey, RationalSurvey and Smart-Survey. These are useful because, ideally, to gauge a serious market response you should ask at least a thousand respondents. Some of these software tools are free, others start at around £15.

YOU'RE PROUD – BUT DON'T SAY IT LOUD JUST YET

At this point, you can start to feel a bit paranoid. You've got an amazing idea, you've tested it for financial strength, you've identified your customers, you know your market and you've had nine sleepless nights on the trot, your brain buzzing with activity at 4am. But it's true – you do need to be careful: careless talk costs money. Equally, you need supporters, backers and clients. Silence is not an option. Who can you talk to?

To get going, list the three key people (other than your business partner, if you have one) who you can really trust to talk your idea through with. You need to think carefully: you want someone who will give you necessary criticism, but not be the sort of person who automatically pours cold water on any new idea. Nor do you need someone, probably your mum, who tends to applaud every idea you have no matter how weird, let alone wonderful. Our mums are indeed our biggest fans – that makes them bad sounding boards, not good ones, sadly. (Unless you're feeling at a bit of a low point, in which case, indulge, but then sober up.) You also need someone who understands something of your proposed business – an elderly uncle with a background in country sports is not, for example, the best person with whom to discuss an idea about a new social networking platform. Ideally, you should find someone who can keep a relatively objective head and contribute some business nous. Frustratingly, the smartest people can miss the crux of your idea, but what they will do is ask the right questions and make you look your weaknesses in the eye. Check that you can answer them in such a way that your plan still stands up should their cynicism prove to be justified (hopefully they will only have pointed out flaws that can be put right, not torn apart your whole vision). Although it's tempting to tell the person sitting next to you on the bus about the next big thing that's going to change everyone's lives – don't. Tell people purely on a need-to-know basis and keep track of whom you've talked to.

Sophie: 'Our partners come to us sometimes, ready to expand, but afraid of taking on staff because they have to reveal their secrets and share their magic formulas. We reassure them that it's a leap they're going to have to take, and that's where legal protection (*IP* and employment contracts) is important and meaningful.'

Talking it out can also change your idea. The Cake Nest is a company that sells through notonthehighstreet.com. Initially, the idea was a mail-order cake business. But when the owner, Abigail Phillips, a former banker who wanted to work from home while her two children were small, was first trying to canvass reviews of her cake, she sent out sample slices to different people. It was then that the idea of a 'piece of cake' stuck. Now her business has the far more original – and successful – premise of sending slices of cake for people's birthdays, special occasions or just as something cheerful to receive in the post.

PROTECTING YOUR IDEA

Focus on protecting the areas of your plan that make it unique. That might mean guarding a piece of technology or a formula with your life, or it might mean protecting your brand's look, values or personality. Qualities such as reliability, ethics and style are almost impossible to copy, but they also take time to build – so when we talk about protecting your idea, sometimes it's as much about sticking to your principles as it is about calling in the lawyers.

LEGAL PROTECTION

- Do invest in legal protection. This could be as simple as keeping notes. We posted our first business plan to our solicitors' office, complete with logo, where it remains to this day, postmarked with the date and unopened, on file, should we ever need it. It costs nothing, so why not?
- Non-disclosure agreements (*NDAs*) signal the importance of discretion to potential partners and suppliers, and penalise them if they break confidentiality. You'd have to sue (or settle out of court, which also involves lawyers), so it might only be relied upon as a last resort, but it focuses everyone's mind on secrecy.

Mark any associated and sensitive documents as confidential on every page.

- *Trademarks* (whether your brand name or logo) can be registered at the Intellectual Property Office for £170 at the time of writing, although the legal work attached to doing this could incur extra costs. You can find out more at the Institute of Trade Mark Attorneys or the British Library Business & IP Centre. Something important to note is that you need to get your trademark right at this stage, as well as all the goods and services you want it to cover, as it can't be altered or added to after your application has been submitted. If you want to add products or services, you'll need to apply again to add more classes. A new name or logo means a completely new application.

- *Copyright* covers literary, artistic or creative work and automatically comes into being when a relevant work is created. It lasts for up to seventy years after the creator's death. The best way to protect such a piece of work through copyright is to make a copy or drawing or take a photograph of it and date it. Should it be needed – if someone copies your article, say – the record will help you to prove that the original work was yours and that it occurred at a specific point in time.

- Design rights. All original designs are automatically covered by unregistered design rights, which last up to fifteen years in the UK, and protect the unique design factors that make up the appearance of a product. If you offer the product in the EU, you will automatically have three years' protection.

- Registered design. You can further protect the appearance of the original product you have designed, but not any technical or mechanical functionality (so how an alarm clock looks, but not what makes it tick), by applying for a UK registered design through the Intellectual Property Office. It currently costs £60 per design and will last twenty-five years from the time of application – but do check the renewal terms. You can also apply to the European Trade Marks and Designs Registry to extend this protection to cover the EU. Costs vary.
- *Patents* protect inventions, specifically what they do and how they work. They can be time-consuming and costly to secure (the Intellectual Property Office charges around £250 to process an application, and you may need to pay for help preparing your application), but are essential if your business value depends on a feature that you have invented. The Intellectual Property Office outlines the necessary criteria and details of how to apply.

Ultimately, remember that legal protection can only do so much and costs more to defend than to put in place. There is more to your business than just the idea – as we established at the beginning of this chapter, that's just the first 1 per cent. Finding and reaching your customers, talking to them, building a relationship with them, having a unique look and personality, earning their trust and growing the business with them – that's what will ensure your survival when the copycats come around. But take legal protection seriously and get the best cover you can sensibly afford.

STAY FOCUSED...

It's easier said than done, we know, but don't be sidetracked by the next big idea once you've had the first. At set-up stage, you can lose focus by being drawn in a million different directions. You'll be walking to work one day and think, 'Everyone is wearing this or buying that, maybe that's what I should be doing.' New ideas are all well and good, but not at the expense of the idea you are already focused on for your business.

...BUT KEEP INNOVATING

Even once you've turned your idea into a business and started to yield some results, you shouldn't stop trying to think of fresh innovations. Every business needs to routinely reflect and check whether it is planning ahead in the right way, being flexible about what its customers appear to need and questioning whether it has the right suppliers or technology behind it.

A great example of this for notonthehighstreet.com is with our product inventory and the technology we need to support it. When we started we didn't know, for instance, that our customers would love our personalised, customised products so much, and we certainly didn't realise the incredible range and scope that our partners would offer for doing that. So as we grew, we found new ways on the site to focus on this. We developed technology so that customers could choose to see any bespoke products and we added the option for partners to add as many images as they wanted, so that they could show examples of how a product might be customised with a message or different colourways. We also enabled them to have as many drop-down and 'free text' boxes as they wanted per product, so that if there were twenty ways to customise a product, the customer could use them all.

Now we're taking that to the next level again, and plan to introduce highly sophisticated but blissfully easy-to-use site tools for customers who feel inspired to customise their buy.

The point we're making is that we never get comfortable with where we are. Even when things are going well, we ask: is there more for our customers that we could be doing?

Everything we've talked about here involves you digging deep and thinking hard. But you need to be a tiny bit obsessive. Without doing the Down and Dirty Test, undertaking proper research and constantly working at the idea to see how it stretches and survives, an idea is just that – an idea. It's not a business unless you embrace what it means to do all of the above and pass the test. We hope you finish this chapter feeling fired up and ready to go to the next stage.

WE ASKED OUR PARTNERS...

How did you get your ideas?

Alex Cooke, Nkuku, eco homeware: 'The idea for Nkuku came from a year travelling through Africa and India. We met so many talented artisans along the way who, despite challenging living standards and restricted opportunities, displayed astounding skills. Our objective became to promote and develop the traditional skills of these artisans and bring their work to the UK. The name was borrowed from a village in Zambia where we saw it whitewashed on a hut. The business plan was jotted down on the inside cover of a paperback, on a lovely beach off Malaysia.'

?

Wendy Harrison, Letterfest, personalised keepsakes and prints: 'I'm a designer who moved from London to north Devon, and wanted to start a small business designing, making and selling bespoke, unique items, using local materials and craftsmen. A friend had a sandblaster to engrave slate house signs and I wondered if the same process could work on curved objects, such as pebbles. Smooth river pebbles were the most effective, so I sourced a landscaping company that used them in fountains and water features and started engraving words and letters. We soon realised that customers wanted more bespoke personalisation so we now design engraved dates and names, which make perfect natural keepsakes to mark all occasions.'

?

Amelia Coward, Bombus, bespoke handmade home decorations: Découpage was something my mother had introduced me to at a very young age. She would give me a pair of scissors and an old mail-order catalogue. I remember carefully cutting out the tiny thumbnail images and organising them in piles. She then taught me how to glue the little cut-out pictures onto large pebbles and varnish them for door stops. After several years of working in the commercial textiles and furniture industry, I was keen to do something more handmade. The Bombus story starts back in 2003, when I découpaged vintage comic strips to a Fifties coffee table. I used it for a shop window display as a prop and it sold within hours. This technique was applied to chairs and a range of homeware products. Customers were keen to commission special pieces using their own choice of comics and vintage papers. The light bulb moment came when I stumbled across a box of old maps. The concept of applying maps to the products grew my designs into a whole new world of customers.'

?

Jim Lockwood, Layer Eight, witty t-shirts and prints: 'Layer Eight's designs are very much formed by the things we love and largely things that make us chuckle. As our products are mostly aimed at men, we are mindful that the notonthehighstreet.com customer is predominantly female, so our objective is to design for "him" through the eyes of "her".'

#3

STARTING A BUSINESS

HOW TO GET FROM ZERO TO HERO

'People begin to become successful the minute they decide to be.'

Harvey Mackay

You've got the idea. You've got the courage. Congratulations. Now what you need to know is how to get from zero to one. How, in other words, do you get from dreaming the dream to the pinch-me reality of your first sale? If you've read the previous chapter carefully (and if you thought you could skip it – you can't – go back and read it now), you will have tested your idea, undergone the rigorous financial exam and identified your market.

One thing we know for sure: you need to be hungry. Drive is absolutely fundamental to success. We laugh at phrases such as 'Work smart, not hard.' To succeed in business you need to do both in big measures. When we talk about drive, we mean that you have to work exceptionally hard to push your business on. And what do we mean by hard? That if you settle for second rate, or catch yourself thinking, 'That'll do', or avoid a task because it's just too difficult, you're setting yourself up to fail. Working hard means facing up to whatever needs to be done.

Furthermore, you need to be sure of what you're doing and completely believe in it. It's this that will give you the motivation to keep going until you succeed. Someone once said to us: 'You may think you don't have stamina or drive, yet if you're reading the most amazing book you'll stay up all night to finish it.' Why would you do that? Because you want to. It's the same with your business – you'll find the push to make it a success if you really believe in it.

For us, we felt particularly fortunate from that point of view. Not only were we in love with our business and absolutely convinced that it was exactly what customers wanted, we also had the knowledge that our concept was genuinely worthwhile and valuable to the world at large. There was potential for a greater good, rather than just for us to be successful entrepreneurs, if we could support the small businesses we knew were struggling to get to market.

Perhaps one of our best examples of this is in the story of Lily Belle, a jewellery business founded by Patroula Waters Coles and Kirstie King, which coincidentally launched the same day that we did. From a cottage industry with modest beginnings on the kitchen table they are soon set to pass the landmark £1 million in sales since they began with notonthehighstreet.com in 2006. They now employ two full-time staff and work from an independent studio of their own.

Before we get going, just one caveat. No one has a silver bullet to business success. It's very easy to look at some established entrepreneurs and think that they have a magic recipe that the rest of us are trying to discover. We have found that women, in particular, often seem to feel that until they have that complete solution they can't start, and it holds them back from taking the first step. We've learnt that no one person has the answer. Building a successful business means you are learning on the hop and making mistakes. You just have to be careful and clever, brave and cautious, all at the same time. But when you find your formula, it's one of the most exciting and important stages in a business's life.

WHAT DOES SUCCESS MEAN TO YOU?

In thinking about what shape your business will take, you need to consider the aims of your business. This will help you not only when it comes to making decisions on where you work and whether you will employ anyone, but it will also keep you going when the going gets tough (which it undoubtedly will, at some point). What is your business for? Why do you want to do it yourself? Is it because you want to fulfil a passion or express your creativity? Or because you'd like to take control of your own time and finances? Is it because you need to work but for various reasons, from children at home to living in a rural outpost, you don't want to be in an office 9–5 or commuting? Or do you need to supplement your income without it becoming your main job? Do you have a strong sense of purpose, an ethical drive? Or do you simply need to bring in extra money to pay for nice holidays, a growing shoe collection or to pay off your mortgage in less than ten years?

These things will help you define your measure of success – whether it's the cash you earn, the way you spend your time, your level of enjoyment at work or hunger for a global takeover. It's good to know this because although there is rarely a final destination when it comes to running your own business, you need to know the direction in which your journey will take you.

SHAPING YOUR BRAND

(We're going to discuss this topic across a few chapters rather than all at once because it's at the very heart of everything you do, and questions around it come up at every stage. See more in Chapters 4 and 5).

What is a brand? It's a small word with a big meaning – one that can feel a bit daunting when you first address the question in relation to your own business. But there's a simple way to tackle it. The true essence of your brand is how your customers perceive you, and that is something that you can control in a number of ways – the content on your website, how you package your product, how you talk to your customers, the magazines you choose to advertise in, even the way you style your invoices, and your logo. All of these things encapsulate your brand, but none of them is your brand by itself. Our head of brand, Sarah Wilson, talks about them as birds' nests: lots and lots of little pieces coming from everywhere to make up the whole. You may hear talk about brand pillars, architecture and pyramids but these are all simply frameworks to help us see that a brand is made up of many interdependent elements.

Even the smallest of businesses needs to define its brand. When you get bigger, you might have to start writing down your brand culture, values and purpose. For now, it will be helpful to sketch out what matters to you when it comes to what your company offers and the way it behaves to its customers. Work out what you want your customers to feel and how you are going to achieve that. As a guide, try to identify six key things that make your brand what it is. At notonthehighstreet.com, for example, our key brand principles are: to be always relevant, personal, creative, inspiring, collaborative and original.

Everything we do – whether it's our customer service or making a decision on where to place an ad – is guided by these principles.

If you can capture your brand within a few sentences, this will help you to explain your business to others so that they 'get' it straightaway. This is particularly helpful for your staff, no matter how casually employed they are. They will be able to respond to and treat your customers in the way that you want, as well as to initiate solutions to problems, if they understand the whys and wherefores of how you make company decisions in the first place.

A brand will constantly evolve, as your business does. You need to make sure there's an inherent truth at the core of what you stand for, and that will steer you as you forge ahead. We were completely sure about our brand from day one, but that's not to say we're not still learning. For instance, how important is it that notonthehighstreet.com is a British brand, supporting British businesses? We know it matters – to us, certainly, and we know it's one of the main reasons our customers feel good about shopping with us – but as we grow and sell more internationally, that question comes up over and over again.

WHAT'S IN A NAME?

Before you can start shouting to the world about your exciting new venture, you need to give your future business an identity. What's in a name? A lot. As far as possible, we would recommend that the name of your business clearly signposts to potential customers what it's all about. When so much rides on the success of a Google search, it matters that your brand name contains a vital component of your business offering. For example, selling vintage children's books and naming the company after the first street you lived in – www.glenshawroad.com, say – isn't going to help anyone trying to find you.

If you're unsure, discuss the name with close friends, but bear in mind that this is one of those things where everyone has an opinion. It can be about as helpful as trying baby names – i.e. not at all. Ultimately you can only go with your gut instinct – listen, then decide. If you want a more structured approach to testing out your company name, put a few friends – who are also your target *audience* – in your kitchen, give them a list of your top five names on a piece of paper (so that they can't tell which is your preferred choice) and see what they think.

Our own name came about from the many email conversations that took place between us in the early days. We weren't actively looking for a name at that time (we were happily using a very odd working title, which we will never share); instead, we were looking for a word to use in our business plan to describe the type of products we would offer. We'd talked about things like 'eclectics' and of course 'gifts', but nothing really hit the mark.

Holly had earlier written in an email '. . . they're all the kind of things that are not on the high street'. But at that point, we didn't realise the name had been written down. It was only when Sophie was chatting on the phone about it with a friend from her advertising days, Caroline Thorogood, who had been helping us with our business plan. Caroline said immediately, 'That's your name. I think you've got it already.' She Googled it there and then. 'It's available,' she said. 'Notonthehighstreet.com and .co.uk too. You should just buy them right now.'

Sophie: 'I got that tingly feeling again – the one I'd had when I'd first heard Holly's idea for the business – clicked off and called Holly that second. She was so excited, she instantly recognised how right it was and since she had the same penchant for accumulating web addresses as she did business cards, she knew exactly what to do. In moments, it was ours. Caroline's husband, Graham Pugh, handily also works in advertising, and he and his design partner, Chris Walker, produced the tag-and-ribbon logo we use to this day. We loved it. We had a name that worked, it looked like it was always meant to be. We had even got the web address – without which a name is almost useless now – and it was all coming together.'

As well as being a great name, it completed our *elevator pitch* perfectly. Other successful names that achieve the same kind of thing for our partners include: When I Was a Kid (children's toys); Giftaplant (sending plants as a gift); The Spanish Boot Company (guess what?); and

AS WELL AS BEING A GREAT NAME, IT COMPLETED OUR ELEVATOR PITCH PERFECTLY.

Biscuiteers (biscuits in a box).

But not everyone's name needs to be as literal. Sometimes it's more important that it says something about your brand values than your product, particularly if you want to grow to expand your offering. 'Virgin' was supposedly suggested by one of Sir Richard Branson's first employees because they were all new at business, but its implicit sexy naughtiness will undoubtedly have appealed, too. It was a word that was also easily tagged on to his portfolio of businesses as they grew – Virgin Airlines, Virgin Cola, Virgin Music and so on. And, of course, there are plenty of brand names out there that have now become so closely associated with their product as to be almost indistinguishable from them, even though they didn't carry an immediately obvious meaning to begin with: Google, Hoover, Fairy Liquid . . .

For us, notonthehighstreet.com works perfectly because it not only describes our brand, but it can run beyond the first idea we had for it. In other words, it works as a name for any aggregate of independent companies (i.e. those 'not on the high street') in any sector. In the same way, you might want to think about finding a name that fits more than your first product or service idea. We Make Hats, for example, is a great name for a company that makes hats, but if they decide to branch out into walking sticks it will lose its relevance.

GOOGLE IT

Important question: can you get the web address (also called *URL* or *domain name*) you want? Even if you're not as lucky as we were – that was seven years ago – you need the name to be something that comes up quickly when the relevant *keywords* are Googled. You could simply Google your keywords before you even try thinking of a name, to see if that throws up a logical way to go. If the URL you want is not available, don't give up – you could still buy it if the current owner doesn't appear to be doing much with it. It's worth noting that someone else owning the name with '.com' as opposed to the available '.co.uk' end of the URL isn't always prohibitive: Apple Inc owns apple.com (as in the global computer company) but not apple.co.uk (an illustrator's website) and the *Daily Mail* owns dailymail.co.uk (the world's most successful online newspaper) but not dailymail.com (the local paper for Charleston, Virginia, USA). That said, in an ideal world you would buy up the URLs of both the '.com' and '.co.uk' tags (you can have them both routed to just the one site). If you have big plans, as we did, there are many more besides – we own hundreds of web addresses.

It's also worth looking to see what's available for your proposed brand name on social networking sites such as Twitter and Facebook. There is a point where you have to stop looking for the full suite – notonthehighstreet.com, for example, is too long to be a Twitter name anyway, so we use @notonthehighst – but do push hard for the critical ones.

WHAT DO YOU DO BEST?

Before you can take your business to the next stage, you need to work out what your skills are. This helps you to identify how much of the business you can do yourself. In many ways, it's a lot easier when starting out to do it alone: one of you takes up less space than two, you own 100 per cent of the profits, and there's no one to get annoyed when you make a cup of tea for only yourself. But it can be harder, too: there's no one to share the big decisions with, you can't stop work because if you're not there, no one is (that means no holidays for a few years), and you get stretched very thin trying to manage all aspects of the business, from making the product to paying suppliers and delivering the goods.

Think which parts of the business you could carve up and hand out – if you're not good with book-keeping, for example, then find someone who is. Could you rope in a younger sister or school-leaver you know who is looking for work, to help you package and post? If you don't have the necessary patience to be good at customer service, do you know someone who might deal with any customer issues on your behalf? Or perhaps it's the case that you will only bring out the very best in yourself and make the business a success if you have a partner.

Holly: 'I knew from the start that without someone who could provide business experience and precision, I wouldn't be able to make my idea fly. Equally, while Sophie was searching for a way to run her own business, she needed someone with the big ideas and motivation to push her beyond her comfort zone to make it happen.'

GOING INTO A PARTNERSHIP

Being in a business partnership can be wonderful, as we would both
testify. We believe heartily that when you hit on a great match with
someone, the whole is greater than the sum of its parts. But we know that
finding that special someone to work with can be as heart-wrenching as
dating. In so many ways, it's exactly the same: you're looking for that
spark, an indefinable chemistry that brings the best out in both of you
and makes you feel as if you can conquer the world together. Where do
you find that person? There are only a very few online business partner
matching websites (more's the pity), and rather fewer bars in which you
could chat up a potential co-founder over a cocktail or two. But you can
start by taking a look at your colleagues in your current job, if you're in
one. Or is there someone you remember working with even several years
ago? Do you remember 'clicking' with someone on a professional level?
Or is there another mum on your children's school circuit who you have a
good hunch about?

We were lucky in that we had known each other in a professional
capacity in the past (when we were in the same team at the ad agency) and
each had respect for the other in that regard. We had also been friendly,
keeping in contact over the years with a call, coffee or lunch perhaps once
a year or so. However, we didn't start up this business together because
we were friends: we did it because we felt we each had different things to

bring to the table and because we were professionally complementary. We knew each other in a business sense and there was a real mutual respect between us. There was connection and trust. We had definitely clocked each other.

Nevertheless, very early on we decided to fill out a detailed questionnaire that would not only make us think long and hard about our views on the direction of the business, and the time and energy we were willing to invest in it, but that would force us, as it were, to be completely transparent about those things as we gave our answers. We strongly recommend that if you are planning to go into a partnership, you do the same. In fact, we'll go so far as to say that if you can't see why you need to do this, that's your flashpoint right there. You have to ask yourself – what if something bad happens? You've got to face these dangers head on.

Here are some of the questions we put to each other:

- What is your *shareholding*?
- Do you think that's fair? Why?
- What's your salary expectation/need this year? Next year?
- How big do you want the company to be?
- How do you feel about risk? How much will you take?
- How many hours per week do you expect to work? This year? Next year?
- Is this level of work OK with you and your family?
- How much flexibility do you want? How much do you need?
- What if one of us wanted to leave?

- Who is the ultimate decision-maker? Do you expect that to be upheld?
- Where do you want the last word?
- Where should the other have the last word?
- What would be your ideal role in this business?
- What if one of us can't work – illness, family illness, etc.?
- What excites you most about this opportunity?
- What's your biggest concern?
- What are your three main weaknesses? What are your three main strengths?

Needless to say, on reading the other's filled in questionnaire, not all of the answers were what we wanted to hear – we had different ideas on the amount of flexibility we personally needed, for example – but the point was that we were able to talk that through early on, and make it work, and we had shown concern and consideration for the other one's feelings.

It is also advisable to have a legal agreement drawn up between the two – or more – of you, which clearly states the shareholding you each have in the business. This might not seem relevant now, or may even seem a ridiculously overambitious state of affairs, but should you become a big success and one of you decides you want to sell up and live in the Bahamas, you'll need this early agreement. Equally – sorry, but we have to mention the F-word sometimes – should your business fail, you need to be clear on what financial and legal obligations each of you has.

WORKING WITH FRIENDS AND FAMILY

It's only natural that you will turn to your friends and family when looking for support for the business. Some of them will even become your employees. Why would you look elsewhere? They are on your side and will give you everything they've got. They may not even be looking to make a quick buck off you, and that can definitely help when you're getting started. But you have to be very careful when employing a member of your family or a friend. If it doesn't work out, they will still be in your life (as they should be) – letting go of your sister as a worker mustn't mean you lose your sister altogether.

Family, friends and friends of friends – the team in 2008

Before you work together, talk it all through. Ask yourselves the difficult questions: 'What happens if either of us feels this isn't right?' And: 'What happens when I think you are not working hard enough, or you feel I'm not paying you enough?' Document your answers and have both of you sign it – this is not legally binding, but it means you have formalised your agreement. You need to know in advance how any conflict between you will be handled. It's almost inevitable that if it goes wrong there will be some emotional drama involved, but if you have already discussed how you will deal with potential issues, you will lessen the crisis.

Holly: 'We've always worked with family. By day five of notonthehighstreet.com, we had Sally (my mum), Robert (my dad), Carrie (my sister), Julie (Sophie's great friend of twenty years) and Claudia (Sophie's sister) all helping us out. As we added to the staff, they were drawn from our circle of friends, from old school pals to one of my mum's god-daughters.'

We can't say hand on heart that we filled out questionnaires with the friends and family who came to work with us. You have to make a sound judgement when it comes to employing those you love. But even so, if we did it

YOU HAVE TO MAKE A SOUND JUDGEMENT WHEN IT COMES TO EMPLOYING THOSE YOU LOVE.

again, we would definitely use some of the partnership questions (as above) as a test of whether the relative-turned-employee situation was going to work well, and add a few such as these:

- If there was an issue with performance, how do you suggest we handle it?
- What three things do you think we should do to move our relationship from a personal to a professional footing? (Can we, for example, agree on how to handle it when I tell you rather than ask you to do something? Or when you have done it, but I need you to do it again/differently/better? Can we agree that there will be times when you are having a bad day, but that you'll need to put on a brave face and get on with it, when previously we would have chatted about it as friends/sisters?)
- Have you thought through the implications of the fact that this might not work out?
- How comfortable are you with the fact that if we're successful, I will have more of the credit?
- How comfortable are you with the fact that if we're successful, I will probably benefit more, financially, than you?
- I'm the boss. How does that make you/me feel?
- You're my employee. How does that make you/me feel?

We think we're lucky in that we have a radar that works when it comes to spotting good people. Nevertheless, we are hard about it. Having family work for you makes business sense – they are loyal, inexpensive (to start with), trustworthy and they give 120 per cent from day one. Plus, they care. But there were times when things got tough and we had to ask ourselves who we would have to let go in order to survive. If you can't envisage that situation, then question whether it is right for you to turn to them in the first place.

LOCATION, LOCATION, LOCATION

Now you've got your name, and possibly your business partner, where are you going to work? For obvious reasons, it's quick and usually relatively cheaper to set up from your home than to rent an office or studio. There are certain considerations, of course. You may not, for example, want your home telephone number also to be the business number (particularly if your child/Spanish lodger/chatty mother-in-law tends to pick up the phone). Setting up a second line for business calls or internet connection is relatively straightforward – check with your telephone operator, but it shouldn't cost much and can be up and running within a few days. It's a good thing to do, as it establishes to everyone else in the house that when that telephone rings you are at work and not just sitting in the corner playing at offices. It also removes the temptation to overuse your mobile and helps to compartmentalise your costs. (Chapter 4 has more on making your workspace at home work for you, as well as being somewhere presentable for your clients.)

If you do not want to work from home, then you obviously need to consider the cost of running a studio or office. Think carefully first about why you feel you cannot work from home. Is it space? Until you have any employees there's only you to fit in, plus a laptop. Plenty of businesses started on the kitchen table (including ours). Even the famous screenwriter and director Woody Allen allegedly still prefers to work from a desk in the corner of his bedroom. If you've got kit to fit in – such as a sewing machine and materials – is there a way of clearing a corner for it and eating your meals off your lap for a while? If you need space for stock, can you ask around your local area to see if there's a garage you could rent from a neighbour or even a spare bedroom? Or do you want to set up outside the home so as to give you the discipline of 'going to work'? In which case, you may need to get real and exercise some willpower. Don't stay in your pyjamas – get up, get dressed, go out and buy a cup of coffee or newspaper and then 'walk to work', i.e. back home.

If at all possible, it's better to outgrow the space you're in and then move on than feel that you need to grow the business to justify the square footage you're paying for.

As much as you probably need to start at home where it's a known entity and cheap, you must have it in your plan to expand your workspace if you want to grow the business. Mark the milestones in your cash flow that will generate the physical growth. We battled between feeling that notonthehighstreet.com wouldn't happen unless we made the leap to take an office and employ people, and putting it off for as long as possible so as to avoid having to pay the overheads. But we definitely reached a point where if we hadn't taken an office, we would have effectively killed the business before it had taken off.

Sophie: 'I remember thinking, "We've got to grow the business up and out." It was a very symbolic moment, taking the office – it marked the difference between negotiating and accepting our destiny.'

Abigail Bryans of Abigail Bryans Designs, hand-painted wooden signs: 'My mother – who is seventy-five! – helped me by painting the slats of wood, drilling them and cutting them up. My sister helped me at the beginning by stringing the signs. Now I employ two part-timers and need to build a shed at the end of the garden to work in, as the business is too big to be operating from my very small kitchen any longer.'

Jo Jenner of 3 Blonde Bears, personalised accessories and homeware: 'I started on the kitchen table, moved to a back bedroom and then to a purpose-built onsite studio – aka "the shed". Recently, I made the decision to move to separate premises. I can see that the business has potential for growth; in order to do this, I need to expand my staff numbers and to do that, I need a bigger space. Finance was a factor, too, as I got a good deal on the premises and had the cash in hand for the term of the rental period. It allowed me to centralise the stock storage and have larger work stations, therefore saving time moving stock around. The location was also ideal, as it's a road away from my house. The risk is covered because we have the money to try out our own premises. The challenge is to trade into the space so we can stay here, or even move somewhere bigger . . .'

A brief word on...

TAX DEDUCTIBLE ITEMS

Working from home can have some tax benefits (there are costs that can be offset as *tax deductible*), but there are guidelines on this. It's definitely worth knowing what's what, as you could benefit financially, but you need to talk to an accountant about what is the best route for you as the rules are frustratingly vague.

THE VIRTUAL SHOPFRONT

In case you hadn't noticed – and we're pretty sure you have – the internet is everything to business now. Even if it seems to have nothing to do with you, we promise it has everything to do with you. You need to recognise that a website and other forms of online communication – from blogs and Facebook to Twitter and email newsletters – are critical, not optional. Think about where your customers will view or buy what you've got for sale. If you are offering, say, a baby massage service at clients' homes, then obviously they won't ever see yours, but you do need a website so that they can find out about you, get your contact details and possibly even make bookings. That an online presence is necessary goes without saying, and there's no need to feel daunted at the prospect of building one. For many businesses, just a single page with contact details on it will do (although we would encourage you to expand on this further down the line). For months before we officially launched we had a microsite, which we built soon after we'd set the date that notonthehighstreet.com would go live, just to let people know we were in town and we were serious. The microsite was a great idea: it was the countdown clock that gave us nightmares. (Chapter 4 goes into more detail about how to build a website and put the right content on it.)

HOW WILL YOU GET TO MARKET?

Where you work does, of course, determine how you deliver to your customers. Will you sell directly through your own transactional website? Or via a shared marketplace, such as notonthehighstreet.com? Could you launch at a shopping fair? Are you dreaming about setting up your own shop? Will you be going into clients' homes for the service you offer or will you need them to come and visit you at yours?

These are the questions: your answers will provide your route to market. To start with, just pick one route, and we suggest that it's a manageable one at that. A huge order from a major department store might seem like a dream come true, for instance, but if it's in your first week, it might not be the wisest start for your business. Over time, you could get to the point where you are reaching your customer through a marketplace, through retailers, in your own shop and through your own site.

THE PAPERWORK

If you're setting up a limited company, there's a certain amount of paper-work involved. There are several reasons for doing this – your accountant will be able to advise on what's relevant to you – but typically, a business would choose to do this in order to limit its financial liability, or to register for *VAT* (and you only have to do that if you need to offset VAT costs from suppliers or if you are going to turn over more than a certain amount in a year). The simplest way is to go to the Companies House website. You'll need to provide a name, address and details of the director (who will be you or possibly you and someone else) and the secretary if you want to have one (you can nominate your accountant or just someone you trust, such as your aunt or brother). If you own the company entirely, then declare that you own 100 per cent of the shares and are the sole *shareholder*. There's a small fee to pay for registering your company, too. (As we've mentioned in the previous chapter, Companies House is also a useful website for checking out other companies similar to your own.) We registered notonthehighstreet.com in November 2005 and, looking back, it's funny to think how underwhelmed we were. Robert sent an email to say, 'Congratulations – you are now a business!' after he had registered us, and it didn't really click as to what a momentous thing it was. We think it must be because when it comes to creating a business, the paperwork is just box-ticking stuff. What's real and exciting is the first customer, the first sale. Which brings us to . . .

THE BUSINESS PLAN

Now you've got the basic structure of your business together – the who, the where and the why – you need to get down to details. This is where you write down your well-researched three-year business plan. You're halfway there already, because you've done the Down and Dirty Test in Chapter 2, but this is where you really knock all that information into shape. It's a big job, but just as some people relish a therapeutic spring clean (which we both love) or conjuring up a home-cooked meal from scratch (which we don't), it's a highly satisfying task.

Sophie: 'Historically, business plans have been my job. I've done a few. The really exciting ones usually start on the back of an envelope or in your head in the middle of the night.'

At the beginning, just jot down a few bullet points. Don't start with a huge document or template to fill in – that will kill it. The headings should naturally spell out why your big idea is great and lead into structure and detail, but at the heart of its thirty-odd pages should be you, sharing with your reader what excites you about your business. It is this document that you will take to investors, personal backers, the bank manager, your parents . . . It will also contain all the information that you'll need to be able to pull out of the hat at a moment's notice when, for example, negotiating with suppliers. Even if you're the only person who ever reads it, don't run a business without one. This process helps you understand every corner and every detail of your business. By the end of it, you're not just best friends with the idea – you're soulmates for life.

Our format for a business plan isn't revolutionary. You simply need to cover the idea and product (that's the opportunity), why it's needed (that's the market), who you're up against (your competition), then back it up with all the research you've done to prove you're right. A timing plan or roll-out will explain how you're going to make it happen and what happens when it does.

What your business plan should include:

- A detailed description of the business opportunity – who you are, what you plan to sell or offer, why you are doing it and who your customers will be.
- The market conditions and a brief review of the competition.
- Your marketing and sales strategy – why you think people will buy what you want to sell and how you plan to sell it to them.
- Your team – your own relevant credentials and those of the people you plan to recruit.
- Your operations – where you will work from and the facilities you have, from IT to pottery kilns.
- Financial forecasts – this shows that what you are promising stacks up when it comes to the numbers.
- A timed roll-out plan for the next twelve to twenty-four months.

There are seven rules to stick to when writing it:

- Keep it interesting, not to mention infectious, information-rich and coloured with your own passion. Start with a headline opener ('Half a million people searched online for a product like this last year, but only one business does it the way ours does, and this is how . . .'). Add the detail only when you've got your reader hooked. No waffling.

- Never lie. Play up your achievements and ambitions, but don't make it all sound like a bed of roses. Stick to the facts, too. If you've had a false start, say so. We'll often throw some already-solved problems into the mix; business is all about solving problems, so potential backers love to see that you know how to deal with trouble.

- Always tailor your plan to the audience and objective. If you must use a template, make sure it's the right one. There is nothing worse than a square-peg-round-hole business plan – we've seen a lot of them. Put in the effort to craft your own, using headings and previous examples to make sure you've got everything covered. Go to Business Link for detailed information on this. The only exception is that some

KEEP IT INTERESTING, NOT TO MENTION INFECTIOUS, INFORMATION-RICH AND COLOURED WITH YOUR OWN PASSION.

banks or financiers may prescribe the exact format they require – if they do, then use it. Don't be scared to be colourful and bring it to life. It's about facts and not pretty pictures, but you can bring a feminine edge to the plan.

- Use headings and bullet points to structure the content. Make it logical to navigate, as it probably won't be read in the order you present it in.

- Back up as much as you can with facts and research, be that desk research or your own customer findings.

- Never forget that a business plan – like the business itself – always comes back to money. Is it viable? Will it take off? When? Spreadsheets of costs, financial results and forecasts are a scorecard of how well you're doing and how soon the venture will actually start delivering that precious, all-important financial return. The money page will be the most read by far.

- Always include a one-page executive summary. Write it last, but put it first to act as a taster to stir up interest. Edit it down to 100 words and that's your elevator pitch done too. This might be the only page an investor will read. Make sure they get it, and get excited.

A brief word on...

QUALITY QUOTAS

We've got just one thing to say here: if you want lift off, you need to get your quality quota right. This means balancing a drive for excellence with the reality of simply getting a task done. In all probability, this means you're going to have to make your peace with imperfection. At some point you have to be happy to say that website or that email is good enough. This doesn't mean settling for second best – it means that what you've got is as near enough to perfect as you can get it for now. Waiting for 100 per cent when 98 per cent is good enough is one reason women don't start up a business in the first place. Sometimes it's more important to get started and get to market. Call it a soft launch, that handy expression which means, 'I'm still working on it, but I want to see how the customer responds and adjust it accordingly.' Whilst we'd never send out something we knew was substandard – far from it – we take great care not to be perfectionists. We can, and do, make the tough choice every day between doing it 100 per cent right and doing it right now.

WHEN TO QUIT THE DAY JOB

One old cliché is true: it takes twice as long and costs twice as much as you thought it would to set up a new business. If anything, the reality is even more extreme: you're lucky if it only costs you twice as much – three or four times is typical.

And start-ups are stressful. If you sacrifice your salary, you only double the stress. Quitting the day job is like making the decision to get an office – there's a fine balance between foolhardiness and giving your business wings by giving it your full attention. Your financial forecast – and whether you're meeting it – will be what helps you decide. If you're on track and a wage seems possible, that's an epic achievement and we would take the leap, every time. (See more on when to pay yourself in Chapter 6.)

WORK HARD, THEN WORK EVEN HARDER

Work hard, then work even harder. (So true, we had to say it twice.) There will be times when your limbs will be almost dropping off from sheer exhaustion. Nights when you've forgotten that getting into bed was what you used to do when the stars came out. Coffee becomes less of a hot beverage and more of a life-saving tactic. You'll hallucinate, imagining that the cold hard surface of a table is a soft fluffy pillow that needs you to lie your head on it for a minute or two. Yes, it will be hell. But it will be necessary. And worth it.

The thing is, all that didn't – doesn't – scare us. On the contrary, it's an empowering thought that the key to success is there to be taken by anyone who has the determination to keep at it. It's the hard work you put in that gives you your single biggest competitive advantage. You snooze, you lose. Malcolm Gladwell articulates this advice in his book, *Outliers* (Penguin, 2009), which describes

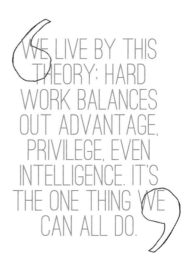

WE LIVE BY THIS THEORY: HARD WORK BALANCES OUT ADVANTAGE, PRIVILEGE, EVEN INTELLIGENCE. IT'S THE ONE THING WE CAN ALL DO.

the '10,000-hour rule': by practising and learning for weeks and years, the potential of the likes of The Beatles and Bill Gates was turned into phenomenal success. We live by this theory: hard work balances out advantage, privilege, even intelligence. It's the one thing we can all do.

If you don't recognise yourself in the picture we've painted then find what does fire you up. (We recommend Ken Robinson's book, *The Element: How finding your passion changes everything*, Penguin, 2010.)

After an article about notonthehighstreet.com appeared in *Easy Living* magazine, six months after we launched, we got a bit overexcited:

From: Holly
Sent: 07 September 2006 11:32
To: Sophie
Subject: RE:

You and me – who would have thought ten years ago we would be going through one of the most difficult things of our lives together – but at the same time achieving things we never thought possible.

XX

From: Sophie
Sent: 07 September 2006 11:38
To: Holly
Subject: RE:

When we ARE rich and famous (well we're already famous) I will tell everyone that it's all down to your amazingly resilient spirit, and positivity, and decisiveness.

Just hope no one ever reads our emails!

xxx

Our first glossy mag special

EXPECTING THE UNEXPECTED

It's OK to fuck up.

Sometimes, despite the very best of intentions and well-laid plans, things will go wrong. And they might even be your fault. The best thing you can do is own up and face it. By dealing with something that's gone wrong with total honesty and as quickly as possible, you will not only contain it – that is, prevent the problem going from bad to worse – but you will learn from it, too.

Sophie: 'Own your mistakes. A colleague at *Cosmopolitan* showed me the value of this. When I was working as an editorial assistant there, I was terrified of messing up, but learned from her that people who are ready to claim their failures as well as their successes inspire real confidence and are most impressive in the long term. This was the *Cosmo*

culture – if you said anything, you said it confidently, including, "I was wrong." But I learned that you didn't ever say, "Now what do I do?" Or, "I don't know." You said, "I'm going to find out how to fix that and come straight back to you."'

PEOPLE WHO ARE READY TO CLAIM THEIR FAILURES INSPIRE CONFIDENCE.

THE CUSTOMER

NOT ONLY ALWAYS RIGHT, BUT AT THE HEART OF YOUR ENTIRE BUSINESS

There are businesses out there who like everything about what they do except for the fact that they have to deal with customers. They don't tend to survive. The fundamental truth is that before you think about anything, you have to think about the people who are buying into your business. Without them you make no sales, you make no money, you have no business – in fact, you don't even know what to do. It's to your own advantage to get to know your customers well and to be on as good terms with them as you possibly can be.

The customer has to be at the absolute forefront of everything you do for your business. Every decision you make has to be on your customer's behalf.

GOOD CUSTOMER PRACTICE

- Before you get up and running, establish rules and practices for your company as to how you will deal with your customers. Think about them in the context of your brand values and what you personally would expect and appreciate as a customer.
- Use technology to systematically manage enquiries (there is software available).

- Set your own standards of service, let your customers know about them and stick to them.
- Clearly display any returns policy, returns address and company information on your website and paperwork accompanying an order.
- Comply with relevant legislation, such as *Distance Selling Regulations*. (These are complicated; Business Link gives a good overview.)
- Aim always to respond to a customer enquiry within twenty-four hours. Set aside time first thing in the morning and at the end of the day for this task.
- Deal with emergencies there and then.
- Keep asking yourself what your customer needs, and check if you are meeting those needs in the most efficient, polite way possible.

Your relationship with your customers can be the most rewarding part of your business, so it's worth that extra effort upfront. It has been for us. We've had a great experience with our customers; many seem almost as excited as we are to have discovered notonthehighstreet.com, so one of our favourite pastimes is sharing lovely customer comments around the office. That just makes our day.

Of course we – and our partners – don't get it 100 per cent right, and you need certain skills to deal with negative feedback. Responding politely to someone who has told you that your product is rubbish – akin to being told your baby is ugly – can feel nigh on impossible. But you've got to do it. Try to remember that they're just disappointed, and we're all guilty of getting carried away when we feel like that. Chiefly, you must let them know that you understand. Ensure you communicate with your customer as soon as there's an issue to be dealt with. Putting off dealing with an issue until further down the line makes it harder to rectify. We've known businesses that have ended up sending out products for free, as an apology, because they didn't talk to their customer quickly enough in the first place.

It's not all bad. Sometimes dealing with something that has gone wrong can actually strengthen your customer rapport, and you can end up having a better relationship with them. There's even an expression for it: 'A complaint is a gift.' It's not exactly a method we'd recommend, but it does mean you shouldn't be scared of talking to the customer when you need to. What you absolutely do not want is a lifetime of damage to your brand.

When starting out, it's by far the best if you can be the one dealing with customer service at the outset. Not only because you remain in control, but also because it is the most valuable opportunity to get close to your customer and understand more about your business. At notonthehighstreet.com we constantly use the expression, 'We all belong on the shop floor.'

When handling an unhappy customer, our best advice is for you to put yourself in their shoes and try to understand their emotional reaction, without getting emotional yourself. If it does get to you, resist the urge to react immediately. Don't fire off a hasty email. Take a deep breath, scream at the screen, make a cup of coffee or go for a walk. All the time you can be thinking about the day when it's not always you dealing with the customers directly, while taking on board that this is the time to understand this part of the business and create a template for the future.

You need to keep a level business head to ensure that the conclusion is genuinely reasonable and fair for both sides: in other words, you don't have to give the customer everything that they demand of you. Whatever the issue is that they have with you, ask yourself if they have truly received the very best service they could have. Break down the cost of rectifying the problem and remain matter-of-fact about it. So the present wasn't quite the shade of blue the customer was expecting and it was for a special birthday. That's not good, but the emotional moment can't be changed now – it's done. Be absolutely sure that you're meeting your legal obligations (again, check these) but once that's done, avoid overcompensating in return.

When we're training our customer service team at notonthehighstreet.com, we tell them to remove the emotion from the story and leave themselves just the certainties. This allows you to resolve the issue but retain a picture of it, one which only concerns the bare facts of what happened. You can also check the legal side of the issue at that point, the terms and conditions and so on, without being dragged into a quagmire of emotional trauma.

Most importantly, we listen to our customers. Good and bad, we know we need to hear it. Research doesn't have to break the budget – online surveys are cheap and easy to do and, if your customers are engaged, you will be surprised how many respond.

In short: customer service is a bit like the Green Cross Code. Stop, Look, Listen and Think.

A brief word on...

LEGAL SMALL PRINT

There are always legal issues for us to sort, from updating our partner or customer terms and conditions to dealing with some new – or newly discovered – piece of legislation. Thankfully, we've usually been able to find good advice from people who are efficient and pragmatic, so we never need to make a drama out of a crisis (in the early days the advice was quite often provided for free by Sophie's sister, Claudia, who is now happily a fully paid-up member of the team). But we remember only too clearly the days when we were smaller and couldn't always afford specialist advice (even Claudia doesn't know everything, though you'd be forgiven for thinking she does), and how difficult, worrying and time-consuming it was.

When you're looking for a lawyer, you'll find there are essentially two types. Those who seem to work for you only in order to create further work and more fees. And those with integrity, who will say things to you like: 'In a word – don't.' (The former will have charged you £600 and sent pages of closely typed paragraphs to say the same thing.) What you need is a friendly lawyer to tell you for free when you need to get some proper paid-for legal advice, and when you can just leave it. You will need legal advice at some point, so ask around as soon as you can. At the very least, go to the Law Society, who will tell you where you can get half an hour of bespoke advice for free.

REVIEWING YOUR SUCCESS

All the way through your first year, but particularly at three, six and twelve months, you need to review how you're doing. We repeat to our staff and ourselves frequently, 'Measure, measure, measure.' This will bring you the clarity of vision necessary to ensure that you carry out your plans effectively. Even now, at the start of every year, the two of us sit down and each write out twelve goals for the business. Once we've really pushed ourselves to agree on those things, we look at how we're going to achieve them. We're then in a position to share these objectives with the rest of the team and get everyone working to the same goal. Even if you are working by yourself, pin your twelve goals up on the wall and keep referring to them throughout the year. Have a timeline in place to achieve them.

One of the best ways to review your success (and let's assume it is success, which is why we like that expression) is to use some of the simple digital and online tools you've got to hand. If you received email enquiries, how many did you get and how many of them converted into sales?

Like it or not, the need to monitor your results will mean you'll have to master the basics of using a spreadsheet, and this is a good time to start. You'll find that you can set up a simple formula that will calculate for you the rate at which your leads are converting into sales as you enter the numbers each day or week. Also, get familiar with tools such as Google Analytics, which is free and can tell you how much *traffic* you're getting to your website or blog – even how much money your site is taking, what pages generate the most interest, what pages are making people leave your site, which products are selling and which aren't. There are also tools specifically for monitoring your competition on social networking sites, such as Twitter. It means you can see what works for them and learn from it.

KEY PERFORMANCE INDICATORS

What you're really aiming to do here is to work out over time what your *key performance indicators (KPIs)* are. This is a much-used business expression you're going to get pretty familiar with, if you can just forgive the jargon. Everyone who has a business should know their KPIs like the back of their hand. By tracking them, you know what to expect, so you know what's going wrong very quickly and can deal with it. Equally, you can see what's working well and therefore know where to focus your energy and what to do more of.

Create a spreadsheet for this purpose and – once you've decided what you need to track – record everything, always, for as long as you're in business. When you grow, you can get software that does this automatically for you, but only a human being (you) can actually look at the numbers and think about what they're telling you.

Typically, your spreadsheet should include daily/weekly/monthly numbers for:

- Number of enquiries/leads/traffic/interactions (how much interest you are generating).
- Number of transactions.
- Your conversion rates (what percentage of your leads turn into sales).
- Sales in £s.
- Average price spend per transaction.
- Number of new customers.
- Number of repeat customers.
- Comparisons for all of the above to last year, last month, last week or all three.

AFTER YEAR ONE

When you've got your first year under your belt, you will be able to congratulate yourself – you've made it this far. After all, 20 per cent of businesses fail within their first year. But you still won't be able to sit back and relax: 50 per cent of businesses fail within the first three years.

Staying ahead of trends and seasonal patterns means your business constantly innovates and evolves – and that's what ensures survival.

But while you're not sinking back into the leather armchair just yet, certain things are so much easier in year two because you will see them coming around again and you can make relevant comparisons. Plus, you should be starting to see some real organic growth, some evidence that your idea is turning into the business you planned.

Holly: 'I remember the relief when the first year was over. Surely the second year had to be better! I see now that we were unrealistic about our business at the beginning: it was, after all, little more than twelve months old. We put ourselves under a huge amount of pressure to be a roaring success from the start, but of course few had heard of us – naturally it wasn't going to be easy. In the end, year two did get better, but it's only now – in our seventh year – that we can see with the benefit of hindsight that there was a pattern of genuine and steady growth all along.'

Getting your business from zero to hero will be one of the hardest and most exhilarating things you do. The satisfaction of seeing a sale made, the money coming in and the praise from customers is a high akin to the feeling of hearing someone you've fallen in love with say they love you back for the first time. It feels deeply personal. And so it should: it's your idea, your creation. At the same time, you need always to be aware that your business has to be just that – a business. It is vital that you are professional and clear-headed about the direction it is going in, what its needs are and how others are responding to it. If alarm bells ring – take heed, and quickly. A business sucks up time, money, energy, focus and drive: make sure it works for you as much as you work for it. And enjoy it! We love what we do, that's why we want you to do it too.

WE ASKED OUR PARTNERS...

**What do you wish you'd known before
starting your business?**

Claudette Worters, murano glass jewellery: 'My sister runs her
own very successful business with her business partner who was a friend
from college. I wish I had found the right somebody to bounce ideas off
and make important financial decisions with from the start.'

— ? —

David Emery, The Drifting Bear Co., bespoke prints: 'How good
it was – if I'd known, I would have done it sooner!'

— ? —

Susan Buckland, Hurley Burley, silver jewellery: 'Don't under-
estimate your potential, and do anticipate success. Allow for this when
planning your future. When we started, despite everyone else's enthusiasm, we had no idea of our potential and no long-term plan. It would
have been so much better had we recognised our strengths at the start and
created a business plan that anticipated growth rather than reacted to it.
This would have made a difference to many things, including investment,
premises, staffing and customer perception. Think about how your brand
name will be perceived in five years' time and how it will look in different
formats. Will you want to work from the kitchen table with staff at 6pm
while preparing your children's tea? All this assumes you want to grow
your business; if you don't, it's equally important to plan your future to

contain it and work on profitability whilst keeping it manageable. All of these are issues we didn't address before we started and have had to catch up on. With the power of hindsight, there is a lot we would have done differently!'

?

Vicki Smith, sgt smith, children's fashion: 'That the point never comes when your company is up and running and "ticks over". Running a business is a constant evolving and learning experience.'

What made you want to start your own business?

Emma Wood, Sweet William Designs, handmade ceramic kitchenware: 'I loved pottery at school and used my annual leave from work to attend various ceramic courses. When I realised it was time for a career change, I resigned from my job and sold my house in the same month, using the proceeds to set up Sweet William.'

?

Abigail Bryans, Abigail Bryans Designs, hand-painted wooden signs: 'My husband left me and then moved to Australia and, as a single parent of three children, I had to earn an income. I had been painting as a hobby, but didn't know if I could make a go of it. A friend said: "Don't be frightened to fail." That was nine years ago.'

?

Suzi Warren, Twisted Twee, witty clothing and homeware: 'When I became pregnant, I entered a retail world of fluffy hell. I soon learnt that my daughter was not interested in cloying sentimentality, but liked bashing saucepan lids together and sticking her fingers in plug sockets. So her dad and I designed t-shirts that paid tribute to her thuggish charms and the general befuddlement and follies of child-rearing. We both took a six-month sabbatical from our jobs as art directors and spent it designing a website we could actually navigate. By the end of the sabbatical, I took the plunge, packed in my job and went full pelt to twist all things twee.'

Patti Bright, Siop Gardd, handmade wooden birdhouses and signs: 'The recession kick-started our business. We needed to find another way of earning an income and we also wanted to make a complete change in our lives.'

#4

LAUNCHING WITH A BANG

NOT A FIZZLE

> *'I'm pretty sure there's a lot more to life than being really, really, ridiculously good-looking. And I plan on finding out what that is.'*
>
> **Derek Zoolander, *Zoolander***

A confession. At home and at work, we are unashamedly lookist. We've tried to deny it but, for us, looks matter. There may be a mug out there that is the perfect size and weight, with exactly the right shaped handle . . . but unless it's also easy on the eye we won't be putting it in our kitchen cupboard. It's not just about being surrounded by lovely things – although that's pretty much a given in our houses and at notonthehighstreet.com HQ – it's about the fact that when something looks good, it sends out the right message. A well-chosen handbag/logo/ gift box/envelope says: thoughtfulness, maturity, confidence. A wine connoisseur once told us that if you don't know which bottle of wine to choose from the over-stocked shelves at the supermarket, look for the one with the nicest label in your price range. The likelihood is that if the makers have spent time and effort on it, they've probably done the same with the wine.

From the very first day, we had a strategy to present the business as a mature and grown-up one (even if it wasn't at all how we felt). This meant not only that even the smallest of potential partners received beautiful folders from us when we sent them information, but also that when we first needed stories in the press, we focused on the national broadsheets and leading women's glossy magazines to give us a bigger platform.

We also realised very early on that our business needed to be big to succeed. That's just the way our business model works. Big isn't beautiful for everyone, but it is for us. The beauty of the internet is that size really doesn't matter – to the user, we're all the same, so that's a good start. If our website looked the bee's knees then no one needed to know that our first office was a shameful exercise in well-worn carpets and MDF shelving.

But with some bravado, cheerleaders, a bit of smoke and a few mirrors, we were in a position to start punching well above our weight and creating the illusion of being a bigger company, and a bigger brand, than we really were.

TOP TIP

Most of our partners don't need to, but some have admitted to using a trick or two to make customers think they are more established than they really are. It's more a question of instilling confidence than trying to pull the wool over anyone's eyes. One partner, The Orchard, said when she started out, she would use the word 'team' a lot ('I'll just get one of my team to check that out for you') when the business consisted only of her. Others capitalise on being small. The Country Cottage Shop always makes sure that every customer gets a personal email so that they feel they are being well looked after. Another, Daisyley, told us: 'No, I'm always pretty honest that I am a new, inexperienced business. When someone asked about wholesale I just came clean and said I'd never done wholesale, and they really helped me so I'm glad I was truthful.'

Brands part two:

BRANDING

Your brand is not your logo, trademark, signature colour or even the name. However, these components all form part of your branding and have the task of representing your brand in a very significant way. Your visual identity encompasses your logo, trademark, design, fonts, signature colours, your slogan (also called your endline or strapline), if you have one, and even your company stationery. Your business image matters – it should say everything without you saying anything. Certainly, when it comes to commissioning any imagery or logos for your business, your brand principles should be uppermost in your mind.

Our creative director, Kate Wright, has been instrumental in developing the visual side of notonthehighstreet.com, ensuring that our brand principles are integral in all aspects, from the typography and colours to the paper stock of our business cards. All of these things carry a message.

Kate suggests that the first question to ask yourself is what exactly it is you want to communicate to your customers about your business. Are you creating a minimalistic, understated brand or is it playful and conversational? Secondly, look to see that the identity you choose is relevant to your market. With so much visual noise in our lives, a brand image needs to be distinct and memorable but apposite. Better design will win the race in a competitive market – Apple is the proof of this.

It's worth investing time and money to develop your brand identity, as you will live with it every day and hopefully for a very long time. Changing your mind further down the line could be very expensive, so work to get it right first time.

WEBSITES

Having told everyone about your business, what will they see when they find it? The most obvious place to look for you first will be online – so you need to make sure your website says exactly what you need to communicate about your company.

Just as your friendly local builder will hitch up his trousers and draw in a sharp intake of breath when you tell him you fancy having a go at doing the extension yourself, you have to be careful when planning to build a website. It does help to think of it as similar to building a house. There might be some corners you're happy to cut when it comes to the interior decorations, but you've got to lay decent foundations if it's to have any hope of still standing in a year's time. That mate of your brother

Our first website, April 2006

may well be an excellent website builder, but if he does it for you as a favour now, what will you do when you need to update the site in a few months?

Equally, finding the right agency to build your site is a critical task. Chapter 1 tells the story of how we didn't get that right first time, and learnt the lesson the hard way, burning up lots of our precious cash when we could ill afford to waste it. We can't tell you which company to use – it's your job to work that out – but we can tell you to write a crystal clear brief or spec, be firm about the budget you have and the timelines they have to meet, get at least three quotes from different companies, and at least three independent spoken references from the one you choose.

WHAT KIND OF WEBSITE IS RIGHT FOR YOU?

When it comes to choosing the right website for your business, there are broadly three types to consider:

- *Brochure sites*. These are the simplest sites. Pages of words and images for your customer to view your products and information about your company. Customers cannot shop from this kind of site. If you offer a service of some sort, then even a single page with a brief description of what is available, together with your primary contact details, will do. But make sure it's a clean design that provides the information easily and quickly.

- Blogs. These are run by you, updated frequently with news, information and/or images, and may also have areas for your customers and readers to leave their comments on. Tumblr, Google Blogspot and Wordpress all provide great blogging systems that allow you to create a blog with no tech ability at all. Your web address will have 'blogspot', 'tumblr' or 'wordpress' in it, or you can buy and use your own website address. Tumblr suits images and videos more than text, but looks great and has a strong community around it that helps promote your articles if they're any good. Wordpress does offer a more advanced system, too, which is less blog, more website because it allows you design flexibility. You would need a *hosting service* for this option, though.

- *Transactional sites*. As the name implies, these are websites on which your customers can buy a product or book a service, using an interactive element, whether an e-commerce shopping basket or booking form. These are typically much more complex sites and you should strongly consider calling in the experts. You can DIY with payment systems such as PayPal or WorldPay for a time, or with a ready-built transactional site from somewhere like Shopify, but as your business grows you're likely to consider something more bespoke.

WRITE A CRYSTAL-CLEAR BRIEF, AND BE FIRM ABOUT BUDGET AND TIMELINES.

GETTING THE CONTENT RIGHT

If you are planning to sell products – whether via a transactional website of your own, or via a partnership with someone else (as our partners do with notonthehighstreet.com), or whether you want to use your website simply to direct people to a shop that sells your things – then there's more to think about than launching a site and setting it off on its way. Bear with us here, because this is obviously our area (selling online) and we feel very strongly about it.

Notonthehighstreet.com works with thousands of partners on the site, but we have turned away many times that number whenever we saw that the partnership would not be one that both would benefit from. We only work with businesses that are all of the following things: good quality, good-looking, good value and completely professional in both presentation and service. All too often we see a good idea that is let down by its

Our site as it looks today

execution. You'd be amazed, for example, at how often someone tells a long, intricate story about how a piece of wood was first reclaimed for a table but forgets to mention its size.

Since the early days, we have always tried to help our partners to bring out the very best in themselves if we can see they have the potential to do well, and to encourage them to review and improve their range as they grow. Our team engages with every single partner before they go live on notonthehighstreet.com, advising them on their photography, branding and product descriptions. When customers are browsing your website, remember that they cannot see or touch your products, but they want to be able to picture what it will look like when the postman arrives. Give your customer the tools they require to bring your products to life from the web page.

A GUIDE TO WORDS ON THE WEB

It's good to write something about you and the business (whether on your website home page or in the 'About' section) but keep it short – around 200 words or so, as a rough guide. You only need to let your reader know a little about what you make, sell or offer and what's special or different about it. You can add what you'd like your customers to get out of what you have for sale, whether that's simple pleasure or to share in the values.

- Keep your language easy to read, avoiding obfuscating jargon and purple prose.
- Key customer information, as we talked about in Chapter 3, should be prominent and easily found.
- Product information can include a 'story' behind it, of course, but that matters less than the price, the measurements, the colours (if relevant) and the delivery options.
- Check your spelling. Check it again. And then – yes – check it once more.

A GUIDE TO IMAGERY ON THE WEB

While the text matters, images are vital to successful selling. Customers browse through thousands of products online and images are the first thing they see – our research indicates that 90 per cent of feedback given by customers about a product page relates to the quality of the photography. It's crucial that your products are shown clearly and in a flattering way, so that customers are inspired to click through to make a purchase. What's more, the fast growth of websites such as Pinterest, where users 'pin' favourite images to a virtual noticeboard, means a great photo of your product could be marketed for free by this new kind of social networking.

Even if your business offers a service, rather than products, photography is a great way to communicate what that is. Just make sure the image used is relevant, communicates the benefits and is of high quality. If you're selling products, the following is what we've learned can make the difference between a browse and a buy:

- Use props. Simple props can give a sense of belonging and a sense of scale, helping the customer to understand it at first glance.
- Create a story. Composing a narrative around your product with props and settings allows you to create a style of imagery all your own, contributing to the establishment of your brand. Be wary of overdoing it, though. Keep it simple and only create compositions for key products.
- Be consistent. Keep a sense of your own style. You need your marketing (that is, everything from your website to your stationery) to be cohesive, as well as inspiring.

When it comes to the photography itself, try to invest in having a professional photographer shoot your products. But if this isn't possible, bear the following in mind:

- Most products look best photographed at a slight angle, rather than straight on.

- Make sure the whole product is in view and that it is placed in the centre of the shot. (Props shouldn't overcrowd the image nor detract from the product as the central focus of the photo.)
- Lighting should be bright and natural. Try to keep a consistent light level across your shot and avoid using a flash or dappled light, as they will only distract a customer's attention away from your product.
- Include plenty of *thumbnails* showing the details of your product at different angles, as well as colour, size and personalisation options. You want your shopper to really experience your product by clicking from one image to another while they decide to buy. Use close-ups as well as longer shots. If your product comes in different colours, include thumbnails of these, too.
- Make sure your shots are in sharp focus. (Blurry shots are not more flattering or 'artistic' when you are trying to sell something, they just make the customer think you've got something to hide.)
- Experiment with different foreground and background focus to highlight any particular features of your product.
- Don't forget about packaging. If you send, say, jewellery items in a box, include a thumbnail image of the box.
- Try out software that can help you make simple adjustments to your images with amazing results. Adobe Photoshop is an investment, but other easy-to-use image software is available at little or no cost. Try Picasa and Gimp.
- Certain products are tricky to photograph. Cards need to be

photographed standing up, with detail shown as well as the envelope (in thumbnails). Jewellery should be photographed against a simple background, with specific details highlighted in thumbnails (e.g. personalisation options, choice of chain, stones and so on). Fashion items should either be worn by a professional model or hung, so that the customer can see the product clearly. Thumbnails can be used to show different colourways, detail and fabric.

DELIVERY (POST AND PACKAGING)

If you sell online then your products will have to be sent to your customers. The cost of post and packaging on top of the product itself is something that often takes a customer by surprise, so you need to make it as attractive and efficient as possible to offset any possible annoyance. There are three key stages to this:

Gift-wrapping. If what you sell is likely to be given as a gift, then a great way to set your product apart from others is in the way you wrap it. Professional finishing touches – such as using double-sided tape for a concealed edge – can make all the difference for the customer. You could include a little something for free, such as tissue paper wrapping or a gift tag, or charge a small fee for a more extensive gift-wrap service. But remember that a complimentary gift-wrapping service is a great way of helping to generate sales, ensuring customers will return.

TOP TIPS

Jane Means, gift-wrap guru and designer: 'Do as much preparation as possible prior to your busy periods: bows can be made and paper can be cut during a quiet time. Clear your space so that you can work on a flat surface.'

Josie Parsley, Fraser & Parsley, bespoke stationery: 'Have the best scissors you can afford and only use them for ribbon or paper – never both! Everyone always laughs at me, but you have to only use fabric scissors on ribbon or you can't achieve a perfectly crisp cut! I tie a ribbon scrap to the handles of my fabric scissors to ensure that they don't accidentally get used on paper.'

Parcelling up. As you were told in your sex education classes, don't forget about protection in the heat of the moment. Whether sending by courier or post, package the product appropriately.

- Use bubble wrap, boxes and padding where necessary. You don't want to bulk out your product excessively (it's not very environmentally friendly), but you must ensure you are protecting the product from damage.
- Address the package clearly. Double-check that you've written the delivery address and not the billing address, and used the correct name for the recipient.

- Include your returns address on the parcel to avoid the unnecessary and costly risk of packages getting completely lost in the post.

Dispatch. Use the appropriate delivery carrier and service, whether Royal Mail or a courier service.

- Where possible, use special and/or recorded delivery services. High-value goods should always be sent via a signed-for service to avoid any issues over loss or insurance. To save time queuing in the post office, you can buy pre-paid Special Delivery envelopes from Royal Mail, as well as print out postage at home (so long as you weigh and measure your packages properly).
- Get insurance for goods posted or couriered. If it doesn't come as part of the delivery service, then consider taking out a general annual policy for your business to cover it.
- If you can, email your customer to let them know that the package is on its way.

THE PUBLIC FACE OF PUBLIC RELATIONS

As a part of our 'looks matter' strategy, we invested a huge amount of time and patience in playing the PR game. It's critical from the start of any business because it's your chance to give your company a face and a profile, setting the right tone from the very beginning. But there's an awful lot more one can get wrong than right when it comes to public relations. In Chapter 5 we write in more detail about how to do your own PR. Here we want to cover the importance of getting your tone in tune.

Having landed your first interview with a journalist, here are a few points to keep in mind:

- Work out beforehand the image you want to present.
- Pre-plan the three key messages you want to communicate.
- Stick to your story. Unless it is absolutely relevant to your business, they do not need to know about your childhood, your cat's illness, your opinion on the current state of world affairs or your love life.
- Never tell a journalist anything you wouldn't write on a postcard. (In other words, remember that everything you say, from first hello to last goodbye, is on the record.)
- Resist the temptation to tell all, just to get the interview. The revelation that you married your mum's second husband will be the headline – not your home-delivery pasta service.

Equally, understand that your control over the story is limited. A journalist – or their editor – will decide how much space to give your story when it comes to publication. And they will make their decision later as to what the headline is. Try not to tell them how to write the story. But you can guide them in the right direction with a well-written, short (one side only) press release and accompanying images.

EVENTS AND NETWORKING

We go slightly against the grain when it comes to networking. There are some excellent networks out there that can contribute to your success . . . but they are like gold dust.

Our view is that when you're starting out in business, you might be better off spending the time at work. Going to a business event should be a rare luxury and you should go with a clear purpose.

Holly: 'Work out who's getting what out of you going to the event. If it's not benefiting you directly, then at this stage, think twice.'

When you're starting, keep an eye out for opportunities to get your message out to the right people, and perhaps sometimes that will mean that you will be a bit pushy at a friend's birthday party, handing your card to someone you think will be interested in your new business.

You might not think it, but it's the targeted events – the ones that are positioned as being relevant to your business and objectives – that you need to prepare the most for, whether you have been invited as a guest or speaker. If you are speaking at an event, they are hard work to prepare for and be at – don't treat it as a day off out of the office (ask yourself: if there wasn't any champagne to drink, would I still go?) – but if you get it right, there are some real benefits.

Sophie: 'I believe passionately in doing what I can to inspire the next generation of entrepreneurs and talking to, say, young adults about what the world of business can offer them. It's just about knowing why you're doing it before you give that time.'

- RSVP wisely. Giving a talk is very time-consuming (from preparation to journey time) and even attending events takes precious time you may need in the office. When it comes to networking, make sure that the door that is opening to you is one that you are looking to go through in the first place. Have a fixed objective and pick the events carefully.
- Gather and distribute information. An industry event is an opportunity to present yourself as a key player in the industry and spread your message to customers or clients. You can gather interesting and impressive material for your website and/or blog.
- Put faces to names. Use the time to build rapport with contacts and get to know better the people you've been speaking to via email and social media. Take away the best of the information for your own campaigns and strategies. At the very least, leave feeling motivated either to try something new or stick with confidence to what you're doing.
- Events can be particularly useful when you're at the point of building a product range, looking for suppliers. Not only can you build relationships, but you can also do a quick audit on the company, gathering informal references.

- If you're giving a talk, prepare heavily, watch people speaking on YouTube, TED and Like Minds to learn what styles work. Even better, do a media training course (some are just a few hours long). Make sure you answer the brief and find out who the audience is.
- Don't forget to use events as a PR opportunity – there may be a press presence in the audience, plus talks are often recorded and streamed online.

THE TROPHY CUPBOARD

As part of our ongoing PR campaign, we're also very proactive in entering our business for awards and accolades. For notonthehighstreet.com, winning awards is a great way to make a noise about the businesses we represent and enables us to draw attention to a whole sector of industry that should have a much higher profile than it currently does. It can be a slog – those lengthy forms and presentations don't write themselves, and they have to be seriously impressive – but completely worth it. No one needs to know about any award you didn't win, after all! We like the fact that putting an award application together gives us the chance to reflect on what we've achieved, as well as setting goalposts for what we want to achieve in the future.

If you win, or are even a runner-up, there are numerous benefits. You boost your own morale and that of your team, you gain serious credibility, and the chance to attract new clients and talent. Not only does the award organiser give you PR through their own announcement of your prize – most awards are sponsored, so it's in everyone's interest to make as much noise as possible – but you can splash the news on your own website, CV and sales material. Some prizes should sit on your site permanently – if you win an award for customer service, make sure it sits on your page with the returns policy information.

At the awards ceremony itself you will have networking opportunities while your standing in the industry is validated, showing your customers and clients that you are the best. There might even be a monetary prize or free services to win. Not to mention that you will have a piece of mounted glass/gold/

We were photographed after winning the BT Essence of the Entrepreneur Award in 2008. Wearing a huge ribbon wasn't very comfortable but the results were worth it

plastic to keep in pride of place in your office or loo.

We keep ours in pride of place in our boardroom. Those awards not only represent the hard work that we've put in, but they support our belief that we are doing the right thing. Certain awards feel particularly sweet.

In 2009, not long after we had launched our first catalogue campaign at huge risk (see more in Chapter 5), we entered for an ECMOD – the leading awards for the catalogue and direct commerce industry. We were excited enough when we heard we had been shortlisted, as that meant we would be going to the ceremony night.

When we arrived, we felt like the new kids on the block. Everyone knew each other, clearly very well indeed, and all the big brands were there: Boden, Cath Kidston, Sweaty Betty, Great Little Trading Co. We sat there, half sheepish, half proud as punch, as the announcements began. When our category came up, we didn't know where to look.

And when it happened, it felt just like the Oscars. The envelope opened and we heard the thrilling words: 'And the winner is . . . notonthehighstreet.com!' We stood up, hugged each other for just a little too long, Summerly cheered a bit too loudly, and off we went, up to the stage. You could almost hear people saying, 'Who?' as we walked past. You'll soon know exactly who, we thought.

There are rules for entering awards:

- Keep it relevant – enter awards that are certain to boost your business.
- Think big – be the best in the industry or the highest you can reach – but balance this with avoiding disappointment (for you and clients).
- Don't waste money – awards can be expensive to enter and attend, so choose carefully.

Just to show you what we mean, here are some we won earlier . . .

Media Momentum Women of the Year

Online Retail Awards Prix d'Or

ECMOD Business Excellence Award

Entrepreneurial Woman of the Future Award

Specsavers Everywoman in Retail Entrepreneur of the Year Award

Online Business of the Year at the Nectar Small Business Award

Management Today 35 Women Under 35

HOME, SWEET OFFICE

If you decide to work from home, as 74 per cent of our partners do – whether in their house itself or in the garden shed – then you need to think about how to carve out a workspace to call your own.

It doesn't matter how small the space is, but it needs to be yours. In an ideal scenario, you'd have your own room. It might have multiple uses (i.e. it's also the spare bedroom or shed), but what's essential is that you have peace when you need it, at times when others might not want to be quiet. Working from your kitchen is fine, but not when everyone else in the house is trying to get themselves breakfast or supper. So ask yourself – will anyone else need this space at any other time? Will I be able to work while my boyfriend is watching a movie? Can I work while the children are playing? Your space has to work with the flow of the house-hold, not against it – otherwise you'll be constantly battling with your family or flatmates at a time when you need their support, not resentment.

Next, how are you going to work? As far as possible, your work needs proper space for you to give it your full attention, and you need to be able to store it away neatly and easily when you – finally – give yourself a break. Those of us who care about how our homes look, care about our work environment. In short, you need to pay as much attention to this space as to the painting of your kitchen cupboards. (If you get this right you might have a new kitchen anyway . . .)

Equally, there will be times when you have to meet investors (whether your friend, aunt or bank manager) and possibly even customers in your home/office. It's important that they see you have been professional in terms of making space for the business. You and your workspace need to look clean, efficient and stylish (much like your hair, as below). If you have a creative element to your business, this needs to be reflected in the way you work, demonstrating that you have a good eye in all that you do.

Before anything else, stand back and look at your home with an architect's eye. Spend time thinking about the actual desk or surface, storage and the technology you need. What things do you have to have close to hand, what do you use daily and what will you use only occasionally? You need to be able to access your tools for work easily. Anything that feels like a jigsaw puzzle to get out or put back in is going to frustrate the hell out of you. Things that fall out and hit you on the head when you open the cupboard door are liable to blow your fuse. If you put anything in storage, make sure it is not so tidied away that it is completely forgotten about.

Keep a list to hand that details what is in each well-labelled box.

Unless you actively choose to continue working from home no matter how big your business gets, there will come a time when you grow up and out. When we did, after years of muddling along and having meetings sitting on filing cabinets, it felt, paradoxically enough, as if we had come home.

In the early years, we had always dreamt that we would make our office spaces feel like a home by having meeting rooms styled as, for instance, a cosy kitchen, a boudoir, a big dining room. We imagined a huge Georgian house in the middle of London – a home which would function as an office, turning the idea of working from home on its head. In the end, we wanted to stay in Richmond as we and all our staff love being by the river. So we've just completed a refurb that makes coming to the office a joy for all of us. We have two floors that are cosy and stylish, just as we'd fantasised, and our meeting rooms have names that tell a little of our story. There's Harry's Room, named after Holly's son; Orange Pekoe, which was the name of the cafe we used to have meetings in when we ran out of room elsewhere; the Corner Cafe, which has been kitted out like a sweet shop with jars of bon-bons and candy canes. Best of all, both of us got our own offices – real rooms, with actual walls, and a door we can open and close at will. Confidential conversations no longer have to be conducted in the car or pacing the street on a mobile phone. We can invite people in to sit down and have a cup of tea, and we have proper space for all the pictures, photos and bits and pieces that we have collected along the way. Sometimes, early in the morning, or late at night, the two of us walk around the building, drinking in the extraordinary feeling that this is truly what we wanted.

A brief word on . . .

COMPUTERS AND PRINTERS

At any stage you're in, technology matters. Get the best computer or laptop you can afford. We strongly advise that you invest in a decent, modern printer – a second-hand one at risk of breaking down is just not worth it. Some printers have the better option of refillable cartridges rather than buying new. A huge expense in our first year was print cartridges. Watch out, too, as a lot of printers that seem cheap have very expensive cartridge refills. More expensive printers can be cheaper to refill – so do your research first.

Check you have the right package on your phone and an extra line if you need it, and invest in great WiFi for the house if you don't have it already.

KEEP IT PRETTY

Buy good-looking box files to make sure even the admin part of your business looks first-rate. Even if you do not have boxes of stock, you will soon build up stacks of invoices, books and paper. (So much paper. Offset Amazon Rainforest guilt in any way you can, but you'll be feeling it.) Make sure you have sufficient filing space. Take our word for it: be ultra-organised and think about all of this upfront, rather than wait until your 'piling system' has taken over the living room floor. If you need shelves built, build them now. We think this is one of the most fun things about starting the business and you should enjoy it. It's just like getting all your pencils and pencil case ready for a new year at school. Do go to Ikea – they are fantastic for home-working solutions. They have desks that fold away and clever storage

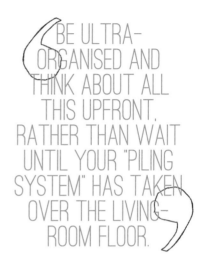

BE ULTRA-ORGANISED AND THINK ABOUT ALL THIS UPFRONT, RATHER THAN WAIT UNTIL YOUR "PILING SYSTEM" HAS TAKEN OVER THE LIVING-ROOM FLOOR.

solutions with draw-down doors so it all looks neat when you have finished. (It is only after six years and three offices that we have grown out of our Swedish flatpack love affair.)

GETTING – AND STAYING – ORGANISED

An organised desk and office can save you time and energy, and create a calming working atmosphere. Somewhat necessary for those days when the phone is ringing off the hook and you've spilt three cups of coffee . . .

- Establish a filing system – ideally a logical A–Z system so you know where everything is at a glance. Review your filing annually, archiving or shredding as necessary.
- Keep a 'to do' file in the front of your filing cabinet, so as to keep a clear desk. This file should be reviewed at the beginning of each day.

- ADD: Action, Delegate, Defer. Look at the paperwork in your in-tray and identify what it is. If it is something that can be done, then do it now if it's going to take you less than two minutes – that's action. Otherwise give it to someone else to do – delegate. Or defer it to do later and put it in the 'to do' file. (But be sensible about this: do not put off until later what can be done now. And use the familiar childhood tactic of eating the thing you like least first – do the worst jobs at the start of the day, don't put them off until the end when you'll only shove them across to tomorrow.)

SHUTDOWN

The most critical thing is that when you have finished work for the day, you need to be able to shut the door, pull down a blind, draw the curtains or close the desk. You need to make sure your work does not dominate your home. It will also cause serious issues if the children pull out important pieces of paper and draw on them, or if you just start to feel overwhelmed because you can see work that needs to be done out of the corner of your eye any which way you look. You have been warned. Believe us: you will be working all the time and it is paramount that, when you do allow yourself to stop, your desk is not whispering for you to come back.

It's not always possible to do this. We know. We fail sometimes, too. But it's good to try.

These are before and after product shots. Here the product (left) was cropped too tightly. The specific detail is less important than the concept of the piece, now better seen as part of a 'story'.

Originally, the details were lost. Now the fastenings can be more clearly seen and the different wording allows the customer to see the bespoke possibilities.

We've come a long way since our first breeze-block offices. Now we live the brand every day.

There's a handmade feel wherever you look, and huge desks were specially designed to bring our teams together and encourage interaction.

The whole place is kitted out with notonthehighstreet.com products, changing with seasons, occasions and trends so that we're constantly inspired by the small businesses we work with.

Anyone who comes to see us gets the brand instantly – where we've come from and what's important to us.

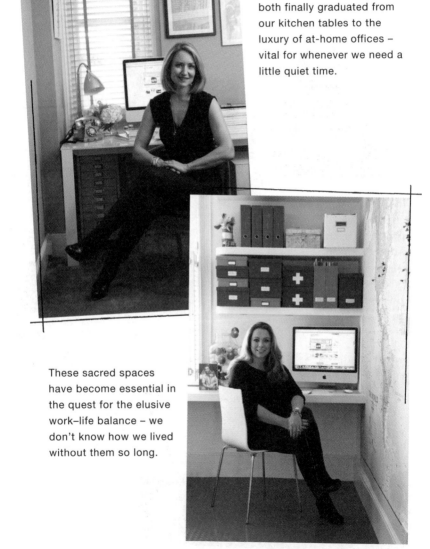

Less than a year ago, we both finally graduated from our kitchen tables to the luxury of at-home offices – vital for whenever we need a little quiet time.

These sacred spaces have become essential in the quest for the elusive work–life balance – we don't know how we lived without them so long.

Holly: 'Sometimes I just couldn't stop working. However late it got, or wherever I was, the urgency wouldn't go away and the brain wouldn't shut down. That's not an excuse not to stop. It's a self-discipline like any other, knowing when to stop. I don't know that all that extra time spent in the darkest hours of the night actually got me any further. If I could do it again, I'd treat my time more carefully.'

YOUR WARDROBE. IT'S NO LAUGHING MATTER

Forgive us, but we have to get personal here. Have you had a good look in the mirror lately? Are you saying what your business needs to say? Because when you are starting and running your own business, you are your business and its best ambassador. Your business and your image need to be as closely matched as a twinset and pearls.

Not only will your looks tell the story of your business in a way that can be helpful when it comes to meeting your customers, securing a better deal with suppliers or landing good PR, but it is especially beneficial when it comes to attracting investment. When an investor buys into a business, they are buying into the people that are running it more than the business concept itself. It matters, therefore, that you demonstrate from the off that you are professional and ambitious. What you wear and how you present yourself can say that more quickly and effectively than any business plan.

Nor is it as simple as dressing smartly. For those businesses with a design element, investors and customers need to see at a glance that you are in tune with what's happening in the worlds of fashion, art and politics. On top of all that, you need to be taken seriously. Your wardrobe is an investment, not a frivolity. We mean it.

Sophie: 'We always made a point of having good clothes, almost more so than now. I remember having a blow-dry on expenses (I wasn't paying myself a salary at the time) because I had a big meeting and needed not to look as if I'd been up all night working.'

Holly: 'I can remember staying up an extra half-hour to paint my nails and iron a shirt, even though it was gone midnight – because it was a highly cost-effective way of looking significantly more professional.'

Amanda Erritt is a stylist and personal shopper who we called in to help us get our wardrobe right when we were first going out to impress the press, to look good in launch photos and then when we went to investors. She emphasises the point that what you say with your clothes is key: 'Eighty-nine per cent of a first impression is based on what you wear,' says Amanda. 'Only 11 per cent is what you say or do. A headmistress client of mine, for example, told me that she needs to strike the right note between authoritativeness and empathy, while also looking current.' Amanda also believes that nothing should be saved for best: 'Every day is best! You need to feel that you can conquer the world. The way you feel when you have dressed up for a wedding or had a blow-dry for a dinner party – that should be the way you face the world every day. Confidence is a self-fulfilling prophecy. Many of my clients have been promoted at work after seeing me. Not just because of the new wardrobe but because it's had a snowball effect on the way they present themselves and are viewed by others.'

Amanda suggests investing in contemporary but well-cut tailoring – trousers and jackets – as well as good shoes, but mixing it with cheaper shirts from high street shops, with quirky prints to show that you are having fun with your clothes. If you've got a very limited budget ahead of an important meeting, you can't go wrong with a pair of jeans and a good jacket.

Patroula Waters Coles and Kirstie King, Lily Belle, sterling silver jewellery: 'Running our own business has allowed us the freedom to dress for work in a way that reflects our personalities as well as the products we sell. Whilst we like to dress smartly for work, we have the freedom to dress in a way that reflects the creative nature of our business. We love the fact that our jewellery complements our everyday working wardrobe and vice versa.'

WE ASKED OUR PARTNERS...

How do you make your environment work for you?

Mat Brown and Laura Marlowe, The Orchard, vintage-inspired garden and home wares: 'I always thought I was an open-plan office type of person, but soon realised that I needed my own space to concentrate on my task list for the day. We now have our own offices, albeit with very thin walls which we can speak to each other through!'

?

Catherine Colebrook, witty British slogans: 'One of the biggest drivers in starting my business was having the flexibility to fit work around a young family. I still work from home, but as the business has grown over the years, I have gone from the kitchen table (literally) to a purpose-built basement. My colleagues are also best friends so I feel completely comfortable having them in my home. During school holidays, we plan it so that we work the bare minimum, but when we do the children have a ready-made club with six of them running riot in the garden. Moving into the basement two years ago was liberating, giving a physical boundary between home and work. Being able to shut the door at the end of the day feels good.'

?

Carol Churchill, Potting Shed Designs, hand-painted wooden signs: 'We started off in a very small shed, just 8' x 6', which was difficult with a resident rabbit (Bumble, our logo)! We soon realised that

134

more space was needed when our business started to grow with notonthehighstreet.com and we built a much larger fit-for-purpose shabby-chic garden workshop (complete with chandelier). We just about manage to run Potting Shed Designs from there, although we do see ourselves having to build another workshop behind the current one to store and cut the wood.

Sign-making from the workshop is fun, as we have music playing and Bumble is always frolicking about. We can step out of the kitchen and into the workshop, which is ideal as we can be preparing meals for the evening in between fulfilling customer orders.'

?

Anne Hyde, Delightful Living, vintage-style signs and homeware: 'I started my sign-making business in June 2008 as a sole trader, alongside my existing full-time graphic design job. Since then I have gone from working in the spare bedroom and a shed in the garden, renting a lock-up for the messier jobs, to a converted dairy on a nearby farm with a workshop and studio. This has meant we can now accommodate three part-time staff and a freelance signwriter when needed. Even more crucially, we are now able to have a clear separation between home and work, which has given us better work–life balance. The Old Cow Shed has a hayloft that hasn't been used for sixty years and, as we grow further, we have the potential to convert that and move the studio part of the business upstairs so the whole of the downstairs can become the workshop.'

#5

FROM CONCEPT TO CONQUEST

THE SECRETS OF SUCCESSFUL MARKETING

> *'Don't tell me the moon is shining; show me the glint of light on broken glass.'*
> **Anton Chekhov**

Marketing. It's a big subject and possibly one of the most hotly debated in business. The desired outcome is simple: promoting your business. But as a catch-all phrase, that doesn't even come close to telling the whole story.

Who do you tell? How do you tell them? What exactly do you let them know? And when? Do you change the message or repeat the key point until they get it? (And who are 'they' anyway?) Should it be beautifully simple or just beautiful? Should you use plain English or evocative, moody language? Do you tell people in new ways or old – through post or email? Through TV or sandwich boards?

So here's the most important thing you need to know about marketing: unless you know who your customer is, what they want and how they want it, anything you try will be about as effective as writing a message in a bottle and chucking it out to sea. Having followed our advice, your research should already tell you how to profile your customer. How old they are/what sex/where they live and so on. That should give you what you need to get up close and personal, so that you know who is buying into your business inside and out. Once you've got into bed with your customer (not literally, but as near as dammit), then you can start to think about your marketing.

There are some who question how anyone can know that marketing works. Surely, it is claimed, if your business is good, that's what keeps the customers coming, not some cleverly designed flyer or viral campaign?

Well, no. We are passionate advocates of marketing. It's essential and it works. We believe that without marketing your business is dead. But there are three things you need to know about marketing, before and after you've mastered the techniques and tools of the trade.

Firstly, it is eye-wateringly expensive. Even those things that are casually labelled 'free advertising' – PR and social media, for example – cost real money in terms of expertise, time and collateral (printing press releases, samples for journalists, creating specially branded pages for your social media fans). More on that to come. And paid marketing is very pricey indeed, especially as you grow and the lower-hanging fruit has already been plucked.

So you must make sure you finance your marketing from the start. There's no point in budgeting for stock and a phone line if no one knows about you: no one will call and no one will buy. But there are definitely short cuts, and we learned a lot about what not to do when we first started.

Secondly, there is no tried-and-tested recipe for marketing, no 'one size fits all' route. What was the winning ticket for someone else will be a loser's streak for your business. And vice versa. It will take time and experimentation to find the formula that works for you. But keep testing, measuring, learning and refining, and you will get there.

Thirdly, and this is the tough part: just when you thought you'd cracked it, things change. One day, the buttons you've been pressing with increasing confidence suddenly don't seem to be working any more. Response rates drop. That press ad, which always did so well for you? It suddenly seems like it didn't even get printed. And so begins again the cycle of testing, learning, rolling out new plans until you find something that really works again . . . for a while.

But don't be downhearted. Your best marketing asset is you. Because you believe in your product and you're determined that the world is going to know about it, you'll roll back your sleeves, hone your skills (and draw on other people's) to work out how. Remember what we said about hard work being your biggest single competitive advantage? Marketing is one of the places you should know that to be at its truest.

One other thing – in this chapter we give a guide to the many marketing channels that are open to any business. Some of these won't seem relevant for a company that is only taking its first steps. But we want you to use this as a manual for the future as much as a get-go guide for today. It's also important that you understand the variety of methods available because, as you grow, you may need to try any one of them at different times.

MARKETING YOUR BRAND

To give yourself a steer on what sort of marketing is right for your business, you need to go back to the first question asked when you shaped your brand: who is your customer and what do they truly want or need? One of the many received wisdoms in marketing is that before you can start marketing your product, you need to be absolutely sure what that product is. That's not as obvious or daft as it sounds, and it might come down to recognising that your product is not actually a product at all, but a brand. Charles Revson, founder of Revlon Cosmetics, understood his brand perfectly when he said, 'In the factory we make cosmetics, in the store we sell hope.' If all goes well, your business idea will be more tangible than that, but it's a great example of the difference between a product and a brand. So what's your point of difference? And how are you going to communicate it? Revson used beautiful packaging, sumptuous formulas, celebrity endorsement, scientific rationale and glamorous advertising to make his customers feel that hope. You'll need to decide what message, and which communication channels – several of which are described later in this chapter – are going to make your customers feel the pull of your brand. Something to be careful of when it comes to marketing your brand is to be wary of doing anything that dilutes it. Not long after you launch, as happened to us, you'll be faced with a round of temptations. We found ourselves almost powerless to resist the instant fix, the one-click sale that might come from discounting, buying customer contact lists and emailing three times a week. All of these cheap tactics would have only served to undermine our brand as one which is aspirational and stylish. We tried a few but, rather like an illicit affair, they never felt right. It was only as time went on and we realised that none of them worked for us, that the temptation went away.

SHOWING OFF

Showing off is a great strategy for marketing. Or, to call it by its more usual name, PR. (In Chapter 3 we talk about the public face of public relations.) As everyone knows, getting mentioned in the national press is any new company's dream. It puts you on the map and – in theory at least – it's free advertising. As we've said, and we're going to say it again later on, there's always a cost involved.

For us, in terms of capturing press interest, notonthehighstreet.com was a very timely venture, benefiting from the decline of the high street, the buzz around small businesses and then the new wave of interest in local producers and farmers' markets. And latterly, as the recession bit, there was a surge of patriotic enthusiasm and support for the small businessman (or woman) holding their own in a treacherous new economic landscape.

The press always liked the story, buying into the point of what we were doing – promoting small businesses so that they could grow and customers could enjoy them. They also liked to be able to put a face and a name to it, and we were willing (if not always comfortable!) to oblige. Each time a good piece ran, traffic spiked for several days on the back of it. This made us fairly shameless in the early days, touting ourselves to win free editorial coverage.

People like to say that we were 'lucky' with our PR and our contacts, because both of us worked before in the media. But we'd reply with that old adage (yes, here comes another one), the harder you work, the luckier you get. And anyway, winning PR is about skill, much more than it is about luck.

The real luck is that we were pretty broke, so PR was all we had. It just had to succeed, so we gave it all we'd got.

Since our launch in April 2006, we have featured in over three thousand press articles and TV and radio programmes – evidence that we pushed very hard and without modesty to get our faces in as many titles as we could, as often as possible. But that's not to say we didn't target some

Our feature in *The Sunday Times* Fast Track 100

titles as ruthlessly as a marksman at a firing range.

There was always something about *The Sunday Times* Business section that got our competitive juices flowing. Right back in 2005, it was the section we read and quoted from in our business plan, the one which fired us up and helped us feel certain we had a great idea when we read other people's success stories, often with the emphasis placed on small businesses and dismal stories about the decline of the high street. We had our sights set on two slots in

Online retailer's homemade success

On the cover of *The Sunday Times* Business supplement

particular. The cover and the Fast Track 100, a league table of Britain's fastest growing private companies. In the end, we got both.

We hit the cover in 2010, after we closed our deal with Index Ventures and Greylock Partners, two of the world's biggest *venture capital* firms. Julie, our PR director, always encouraged us to aim high, so when we said we'd like to break the story there, she agreed. But even after they said they'd take the story, we still couldn't be sure we'd get the cover. On the Sunday we hoped we'd made it in, we were each up and out at the crack of dawn to get the paper. There was no chance of nonchalantly carrying the paper home to check it over the scrambled eggs and coffee. If it happens for you as it happened for us, you'll be ripping off all the plastic in the newsagent, frantically rifling through the sections, hoping you'll find what you want.

There it was. Bold as brass. A big picture of the two of us, slap bang in the middle of the cover, surrounded by beautifully wrapped goodies from notonthehighstreet.com, artfully piled high, and a report of the investment deal to match. It's on our office wall to this day.

The Sunday Times Fast Track 100 was a longer campaign. Over the years, we became a little obsessed with getting listed. We would deliberately leave the supplement lying around in our office for weeks every year when it came out, tormenting ourselves with our absence from it. The trouble was, you had to be invited. Looking back, we realise how unrealistic we were, and yet . . . we weren't. In 2011, we got a call out of the blue: the judges were coming in to meet us.

They arrived, probably only planning to ask us a couple of questions. But this was not an opportunity that we were going to allow to pass by. We did the presentation of our lives. The rankings *The Sunday Times* judges have devised are based on

> IF IT HAPPENS FOR YOU AS IT HAPPENED FOR US, YOU'LL BE RIPPING OFF ALL THE PLASTIC IN THE NEWSAGENT, HOPING YOU'LL FIND WHAT YOU WANT.

financial performance – the level of growth over a time frame – so their meetings typically would ask questions about the P&L, revenue, top line turnover and so on. But we turned it into 'The Holly and Sophie Show', resplendent with an impassioned speech about our purpose as a business and the remarkable ways to personalise a product. They left joking that they'd like to come and work for us.

Holly: 'On the day the results came out, Sophie was out of the country so it was all down to me to get the paper and deliver the news. One problem: I couldn't find my glasses. So little Harry, just learning to read, was charged with the task. He slowly began the inspection of the chart – looking for one of his first words – notonthehighstreet.com. It took a while as it had seemed most realistic to have him start at the bottom. He moved from the long list, having read all the way from a 100 to eleven and saying that he couldn't see it, onto the shorter list, from ten to one. "Don't be silly, Harry," I told him. "It's not going to be there – you need to look again." "No," he said, confidently, "there it is, number nine." After all those years, we'd gone straight into the top ten. We were the only retailer in the shortlist and the only female-led company, too.'

When it comes to the brass tacks of PR and how to do it yourself, we've learned some lessons. First of all, as a start-up company on a small budget, it isn't necessary to take on a PR agency – you can do it in-house to equal effect. Get some expert advice if you can – we had that from Julie – then you can do many of the hard yards yourself. In this way, PR can be one of the most effective and economical methods of reaching mass audiences, raising brand awareness and increasing sales, as well as providing an excellent opportunity to showcase your products/services to your *target demographic* without paying for advertising. It can also give *reach* to any advertising campaign you are running at the same time. What's more, a portfolio of press cuttings is a good way to demonstrate your company's appeal if looking for investment in the future. But you've got to get it right.

When we started out, print and broadcast PR was what we were particularly after – and that's still critical – but increasingly it's online PR coverage, in the form of blogs and online publications, that has a substantial impact on our business. We'd urge you to master the art of both.

Far from happening by magic, a successful PR campaign takes a huge investment in people (your press office and expertise, which might be just you in the early days), patience (because in 100 tries at winning coverage, maybe one will succeed) and professionalism (to get the media to take you seriously).

Features and news journalists are always looking for a story so, above all that, you do need something to say. To that end, one of our very first projects was to conduct and publish our own small business market research so that we had something to talk about in our PR campaign. Then we presented it to the media, the government and captains of industry. By the end of the first year, we had appeared in almost every national newspaper, supplement and women's glossy magazine.

Shopping page journalists are always looking for new and exciting products to feature in their publications. They are drawn to products that have a good *price point*, are photographed well and have a unique selling proposition.

Turnaround time is equally important: some publications work to extremely tight deadlines (an online magazine or a newspaper may need a product and its information within a matter of hours if it's for the following day's edition) and, as with the monthly glossies, some may work up to four months in advance. Your product needs to be developed, made and photographed in time for a relevant publication's planning stage. And you should think about things such as seasonality – a journalist is not going to be interested in a woollen scarf when preparing for the August edition, even if she is working on it in the chilly months of spring.

The formula is simple when you get down to basics. Target the right publications; find interesting, relevant stories to share; have good photographs; and be fast and 100 per cent reliable.

To find the right publications, buy as many as your wallet and arms can handle and find the section that would be most relevant to feature your product or service. Don't forget local and regional titles, especially if your business serves your immediate area. Not only can the coverage be easier to win, but you can really tailor it by, for example, offering a relevant promotion and linking with an event. Keep a folder of tearsheets, to remind you. Don't go for overkill – targeting four or five publications properly is better than sending the same letter out to fifty (not to mention that journalists can smell a round robin email before they've even read it, and they'll more often than not delete it). To find out who is responsible for the section you want to write to, look for the list detailing the staff at the front of the magazine; you will usually find their contact details here, too. You can also often find names and job titles by searching online, and if you really can't find them, call up and speak to an editorial assistant.

Don't forget online publications, too – articles and well-read blogs will sometimes have a higher readership than their offline counterparts. Include them in your sights. Give over plenty of time to trawl the internet, researching and learning about who is looking at what. This is where numbers do matter. You're trying to generate as much interest and traffic as possible, so the sites with the most users are the ones that are most worthy of your time.

Once you've identified who you think will be interested in your offering, then get your story right. What's new about what you've got to say? Why does it fit their publication? (Just because they've written about a very similar item recently, by the way, doesn't mean they'll be interested again. In fact, they're less likely to write about, say, the resurgence of Toby jugs twice in six months. Look instead for a similarity of genre.) Explain briefly but in as compelling a way as possible why your story would be great for them. If they often write about independent sellers, then tell them that you're one. Or if they have a regular page featuring kitchen gadgets then let them know about your all-in-one garlic peeler and apple corer. Be prepared to go beyond the product – it may be that the most interesting thing about you for a magazine feature is not so much your handmade linen napkins or your cookery courses, but the fact that you set up the business after being made redundant from your job as a lollipop lady. (But keep your private life private.)

Next, present the story in the best way possible. That means a good photograph and a clear product description written beneath: name, price, dimensions, colours, where to buy. Include your contact details for further information here, too, even if you've written them on the letter or email. Check the spelling. Check it again.

GUIDE TO WRITING PRESS RELEASES

Generally, keep press releases short and relevant, and to one page where possible. As a rough guide, the standard format for press releases is as follows:

- Date and *embargo*: If it is OK for your news to be reported immediately, put the date you are issuing it and the words 'For Immediate Release' at the top of the page. If you are sending your press release under embargo, write 'Embargoed until' and the date you want the news published.
- Headline: Keep it short and snappy to grab the journalist's attention.
- First paragraph: Follow the 'who, what, why, where, when' rule. This is the key paragraph to get your message and information across.
- Next couple of paragraphs: Expand on the above, working up your key messages, and go into more detail, putting the most important

information first. Include statistics if you have them, highlight your point of difference, what's new, any unusual angle and other interesting, relevant facts. You can also include a short quote to further explain your news and what you are doing. If it's about a new product launch or range, add information such as price, colours and sizes available, availability date and how to buy or order.

- Company information: This is a standard background paragraph about your business at the end of the release: where your company is based, when it launched, what it does, its products/services, who it's run by, any achievements etc. You can use this paragraph time and again. Include the web address for your business here.
- Note to editors: If you are available for interview and/or have photographs you can supply, then say so. Include all your contact details: your name, company name, email and telephone (mobile and landline).

Once you have sent out your press release, you'll need to be available, contactable and quick to respond when a journalist gets in touch.

Most PR is conducted online now (whether by email or through a website), but if you are posting a letter, print it on good paper and send it in an eye-catching envelope. If you are sending a sample of the product, then don't expect it to be returned unless you specifically request it and include an SAE. (We don't recommend sending expensive samples – and they're all expensive if you're giving them away – unless you've already arranged to do so. Just add that 'samples are available upon request'.) If emailing, make sure your photograph is sent in a *low-res* format – no need to clog up their inbox. Just make it clear that you can provide a *hi-res* image if necessary.

To target online blogs and publications, you can also produce content – articles or news stories – then send it to them to use in return for including a link to your site. Major sites are unlikely to be interested in unsolicited content, but smaller ones are always looking for new material so, as long as it's good, there's a chance they'll publish it. (More on blogging below.)

Finally – have you got the timing right? Not just for the publication (as a rough guide to planning times: from one to two weeks ahead for a daily publication, four to six weeks for a weekly, three to four months for a monthly), but for you. Don't make a big noise about your business and then go away for a fortnight, or have no stock to sell, or not have your website ready (as we did). Keep your phone and email switched on and be ready to respond quickly and professionally to any enquiries.

If you don't have any success first time, don't worry. Try and try again. Journalists are frequently overloaded with stories. They may file away your story and come back to you when they're planning a feature that suits it. Follow up your letter or email with a quick telephone call a week or so later, but don't hound them. If you know they're right for you, then keep them informed and send updates on products every couple of months or so. If you've tailored your story in the right way for their publication, that will impress them and should ensure at least a response, even if it's not always the one that you want. Establishing and developing relationships with the key journalists for your business is just as important as placing a specific story.

PR sits under the vast marketing umbrella as a division all of its own, but it is different from the rest, as you are asking a journalist to talk to your customers for you; other marketing methods mean you talk to your customers yourself. Marketing media and communication channels, broadly speaking, are divided into two main areas: on the internet (online marketing) and not on the internet (offline marketing). Each of these has several subplots, and each of those has a different way of working, and its own pros and cons. Don't start them all at once – different customers like to be communicated with in different ways. Some are big fans of Facebook, others wait for a catalogue to browse over with a glass of wine. You need to work out which of these is best for you, your business, your brand and your budget, then introduce one at a time so that you can get an idea of what's working and what's not.

ONLINE MARKETING

All businesses in the twenty-first century, whether they are centred around a transactional site or not, need to plan their marketing online and make it their priority. The world is online, and for a company to have a significant presence in any marketplace it not only needs to be easily found by search engines, but to be at the centre of the right social media networks. Customers will discuss your products, retweet your tweets, 'like' you on Facebook and 'pin' your best images on Pinterest. Being in the middle of these conversations means you can get your message across to customers in a direct, informal and up-to-the-minute way. Loyalty is improved and their experience of your brand becomes a more rounded one. But to do this takes time and money. You need to

ALL BUSINESSES IN THE TWENTY-FIRST CENTURY NEED TO PLAN THEIR MARKETING ONLINE AND MAKE IT THEIR PRIORITY.

make sure you are controlling the conversation in the right way, that you are talking to the right people and that you are responding at the right time.

EMAIL MARKETING

How it works: *Email marketing* is a way of reaching out to customers, both existing and prospective, so long as you've designed an appealing and legal way to capture the email addresses. It's possible to buy lists of email addresses to build up your database, which, while being useful for small businesses who want to grow quickly, should be done with great caution or your mail could end up being treated as spam. Better to grow your own *subscriber list* from people who have chosen to be contacted by you. It's a great way of driving traffic for business, particularly if you include easy calls to action, e.g. a *hyperlink* to your website and a limited-edition product. You must make sure that any data you hold is in line with data protection laws.

Pros: It's quick, inexpensive and direct. The main advantage is that you can trial and test various subject lines, then different creative routes and promotions – right down to the size of your headline – in order to fine-tune how you use email marketing. There are a number of online tools, such as Campaign Monitor and companies such as Emailvision, to help you get started with a professionally run campaign. They will help you organise your *distribution lists*, create a professional-looking mailing and monitor *open rates*.

Cons: It only works if you have a clear strategy. Your subject line needs to be engaging in order to get people to open the email in the first place, and response rates are best when the people you're emailing know you and want to hear from you.

BLOG

How it works: A blog is a website where people regularly record their news, opinions and information. If you do it yourself, it's a great way of bringing your business to life for your customers, whether you write a diary about the day-to-day running of it, or talk about products you're developing or a behind-the-scenes aspect. You can also put up images or quotes that inspire you, bringing your customer closer to you and your company's values. Linking a blog to and from your website, your own email signature strip and social media channels help generate a readership so that it can steadily grow. You do need to update it regularly, posting articles and sending your content to other bloggers you've identified as useful, even giving them permission to use your content so long as they credit you and link back to your blog. (This can also help with *search engine optimisation*, as below.) It's easy to add in tools for customers to post comments, which can build a community around your business.

Pros: Being such a personal thing, a blog is a chance for you to present you and your company with real personality. You can even make a little money out of it if you join a network such as Google Adsense, which will then show ads on your site.

Cons: If you go too off-piste in your blogs, you risk diluting or confusing your brand message. They require a lot of maintenance: you need to identify carefully what your content strategy is – the kinds of things you'll talk about. Who can contribute? What types of articles will you write? Make a commitment to how many articles you will publish in a month, so readers know what to expect. It takes time to write a compelling article and many a blogger has found that initial enthusiasm wears off quite quickly, which can be a disappointment to followers.

FACEBOOK

How it works: Having a company Facebook page (note: a 'page' is a different thing to an individual's account) is a great way of talking to your customers socially. If you were able to gather all your most loyal customers in a bar for a quick drink and a chat, you'd do it, wouldn't you? Facebook is probably the next best thing. You have to be careful how you present yourself, however. The conversation needs to feel real, but at the same time it won't work for your business unless you have worked out just how you want to use it. To share new products? Or news? Or find out more about your customers?

Pros: You're talking to fans of your product and it's a great way to keep them up to speed with what you're doing in an informal way. It's a good way of testing new ideas out without having to commit to them. It's relatively cheap to have a custom-made page designed, so that it feels like part of your brand, and that can also give you better control over its functionality.

Cons: Comments can be negative as well as positive. You need to have a strategy to deal with them – what will you respond to and within what time frame? Make sure you address negative issues so that the fan base can see that any complaints are being dealt with, even if you take the conversation elsewhere to do so.

TWITTER

How it works: Twitter is a social media phenomenon of our time. It's huge – over 300 million users worldwide, with 1.6 billion search queries a day – and yet it is simultaneously able to be very small and personal. In your 140-character 'tweets', you can talk directly to customers, but also to peers and influencers about more than just your business. It's great for giving a very quick response to relevant events, so that followers can see that your business is tuned in. There are free tools available – TweetStats and TweetEffect to name but two – which can help you find out who the key influencers are for existing Twitter users and your competitors. You can also learn when the best times are to tweet, how often, who the top followers are, what tweets resulted in more followers, which made people stop following you and so on.

Pros: It's quick and targeted, a lively way to grab fans' interest with updates and news, as well as allowing you to join in conversations with others about trending topics relevant to your business.

Cons: Some businesses use Twitter as part of their customer service tools, but this necessitates a commitment to get back to people quickly. Make sure you can respond in a timely fashion if you want to use Twitter this way. To manage the amount of attention you give it, designate times of the day to do your tweets. You need to keep up – think of it as a twig in your brand's bird nest – but you have to keep it in its place. Be mindful that word spreads like wildfire on Twitter, so every tweet should be considered as carefully as you would consider a personal email to a customer.

KEEP UP – BUT KEEP IT IN ITS PLACE.

TOP TIP

If you use Twitter, Facebook, Pinterest and have a blog, remember to cross-promote between the four of them. Most blog platforms provide buttons that you can add to your page allowing readers to share its content. Sites such as AddThis offer a range of button tools to share across Facebook, LinkedIn and other channels.

PPC (PAY-PER-CLICK) ADVERTISING

How it works: The most common *PPC* advertising is found in the results of Google when you do a search. The results that appear in the top yellow box or on the right-hand side of the screen are PPC ads and can be bought by anyone with a Google Adwords account. For Bing and Yahoo! go to the Microsoft adCenter. Every time a user clicks on your ad you will have to pay (hence 'pay per click'). This amount is decided by a live online auction and can vary in cost from a few pence to over £20, depending on the industry you are targeting. To get your ad to show, you choose a selection of keywords (e.g. 'dog grooming' or 'baby massage') that you would like your ad to appear for when a user types these into the search engine. You then put these into your Adwords or adCenter account, along with your chosen ad text. You can control how much you would like to bid and your total budget. The higher you bid, the more likely it is that your ad will appear at the top of the results. The most important thing to track is how successfully the keywords are converting to sales. It's one thing to get a click-through to your site, another for that visitor to buy something, and that's the real test of whether PPC works for you.

Pros: PPC is a great way of kick-starting a new business when your website is new, or you don't currently appear within search engines naturally (through search engine optimisation). The ability to control spend closely (because you set the maximum price you pay per click, as well as an overall spending limit), plus the ability to find potential new customers, means PPC should be one of the first online channels to consider.

Cons: PPC is not a simple thing to get working well, and has the potential to spend all of your budget without bringing a return. It is worth learning as much as possible about ways to target your customers or you can get advice from a specialist agency. You have to be prepared to spend money during testing phases, which will be necessary while you refine your targeting and may not bring the return you want initially. Generic keywords are often the most expensive per click (e.g. a search for 'gifts' as opposed to 'gifts for a 90-year-old grandmother').

SEO (SEARCH ENGINE OPTIMISATION)

How it works: Google, Bing and Yahoo! are all search engines. Any time you type in keywords for a search, you get two types of results: paid and 'organic' or 'natural'. *Paid results* are obviously those which are advertisements – that's PPC, as described above. *Organic results* are listed in the order that the search engine has decided is relevant to your enquiry. How the search engine actually makes this decision is a closely guarded secret, and it is constantly tweaked and changed so that no one can second-guess it. But as a general rule, it scans websites searching for the presence of the keywords. It also rates a website that is recommended by others and searches for images and video clips, believing that these things mean a website is a good one. Social media shares – such as Facebook 'likes' – can also boost your results.

As a company, you will want your website to come high up in the results list. The best way to do this is to make your site as relevant as possible to your keywords. You do this through *SEO*, a relatively new marketing tool, which has become something of a dark art. There are agencies that will help you with your SEO, but they can never guarantee you a number one spot in the results listings. As with PPC, the more generic your keywords, the harder it is to come high up.

Getting the spot you want can take months or even years if you are in a very competitive field. Work on producing a great, easily navigated and relevant website for your business, and it should achieve good search engine results on its own merits. Trying to unnaturally gain a higher spot by, say, plastering your keywords all over your website like a wallpaper pattern, can mean that the search engine dismisses your site as 'spam' and blocks it from the results list altogether.

Pros: SEO will probably be the biggest and most consistent driver of traffic to your website. As a new business, a focus on achieving a high ranking naturally means that you will end up with a site that is rich in relevant content. A win-win situation.

Cons: It's a crowded and competitive field. Agencies can be paid to boost a site's position by advising you on optimisation tactics, such as homing in on keywords. SEO can be expensive and time-consuming with no guaranteed results.

AFFILIATE MARKETING

How it works: Affiliate programmes allow you to reward other websites for delivering sales to your business by paying them a commission for every sale delivered. The websites do this by displaying your *banners* on their site. This can be done via a number of UK affiliate networks (including TradeDoubler, Affiliate Window, LinkShare, Commission Junction and Webgains), who manage the payment of commissions and reporting on your behalf. You provide the ad banners, which are then embedded with a code that can automatically track customers who click on them. Usually you only pay websites who deliver sales, but some prefer you to pay on a 'per click' basis.

Pros: *Affiliate marketing* is a great way to kick-start a new business, as you are only paying commissions or charges on sales you have received. This model means you get free advertising (as websites will display your banners on their site, but you pay nothing if customers only see it, or do click but don't purchase) and costs only result from sales.

Cons: You need to keep a close eye on costs and keep negotiating the best terms possible. There are often monthly management costs, too, although these are not usually prohibitive. Be aware of which sites are promoting your business – they should be right for your brand.

DISPLAY ADVERTISING

How it works: This is a broad term for any advertising that uses the display banners that you see across the web. Newer *display advertising* includes *retargeting* (also called 'remarketing'), which means a user is shown relevant ads for your company after they have visited your site, even if they haven't bought anything. (Have you ever looked at a dress or two on an online clothes store, then left the site to read an online magazine instead and noticed that the banner ads on the side were showing the exact same dress from the shop you were just looking at? This is why.) Retargeting campaigns can be run via a number of specialist companies, including Struq and Criteo, or you can run them on the Google Display Network (via a standard Google Adwords account).

Pros: Costs can be controlled and capped. Retargeting can be very effective in persuading a customer to return to a site and make a purchase.

Cons: Standard display can be wasteful when you pay per view and not per click, because although you choose the most relevant places you can,

Our gift guides through the years. Since 2008, over 13 million catalogues have landed on doorsteps across Britain.

A selection of articles
and screenshots that
we've accumulated
over the last six years.
These are just a few
favourites that mark
real milestones for us.

Each week, thousands of people receive an email newsletter from us. Packed with ideas and gift inspiration, they introduce customers to new partners and products, themed around the latest trends or occasions.

2008   2009   2010   2011   2012

there will be cost without clicks to your site. It needs to be done generally to support a wider online marketing package, which is more effective at bringing direct sales.

N.B. Do ensure, whichever method you use, that you comply with the relevant digital legislation.

A brief word on...

PERFORMANCE TRACKING

Google Analytics is used by many bigger businesses in preference to expensive software, because it's so good. Use its training programme and you'll learn all about your website traffic, conversion rate and much more – all for free. Alexa is just for fun – it will give you a steer on how your site is faring in comparison with your competitors. Which reminds us.

Don't do anything you can't measure.

One of the things we avoid like the proverbial plague is any marketing you can't measure. Or at least, we do now. Having had a good chunk of our professional lives in *above-the-line advertising* (print, radio and TV), we gained a Rolls-Royce training in building brands, but it was at a time when no one ever measured anything very much. The internet is a very different thing. Everything is, and should be, measurable. The way we see it is that we'll never have enough money to do all the things we can track and prove, so why would we spend it on things we can't?

OFFLINE MARKETING

Something we learned early on as a business was: don't let the medium take control.

We are an online business – our shopfront is a website – and in this still-feels-sparkling-new digital age, it's easy to forget that one's customers are real people, living in real homes, who still love to hold something in their hands, flick through the pages of a catalogue, stick a Post-it note on it to drop hints to their husbands, or tear out a page and stuff it in their handbag. When we built our catalogue campaign, everyone was saying paper was dead and cyberspace was the only place to be, but we just knew in our hearts that it wasn't true.

Two years after we had launched notonthehighstreet.com, we decided we needed to produce a catalogue. This was something that was not only going to cost us a huge amount of money and risk – the paper and mailing costs alone came to more than our entire first year's marketing budgets – but also involved an enormous amount of extra work. As well as taking on production logistics that were almost biblical in scale, we created a whole new way of producing a mail-order catalogue as a co-operative, by selling advertising space in the pages, as a magazine does. Whispering in our ears all the while were the voices that said paper was dead. And our partners, of course, were counting on us to make it work.

It did.

The first *direct mail* catalogue landed on people's doormats in October 2008, to catch the early Christmas market, and it was as if a

The 2008 gift guide, our
first direct mail catalogue

switch had been flicked. Overnight the orders poured in. We had then, as
we still do, a live record of sales on our order system and there are times
– of which this was one – when we are as glued to it as to a thriller on TV.
Our monthly *turnover* tripled. One day, just a few weeks later, we knew
there was a chance that that night we would hit our first million of the
year. It was a long night – sales slow down after about 10.30pm – but we
were glued to our dashboard, watching it tick round.

Sophie: 'Holly was at home with Frank in Chiswick, tiptoeing to the computer upstairs so as not to wake little baby Harry. I was down the road in Teddington, tucked up in bed with Simon, laptop open, refreshing the screen every few minutes. Holly and I were texting each other constantly.'

When that magic figure hit, so did the reality. All that hard work had come to something. It was really happening. It's one of our happiest memories. And all because we didn't let the medium take control.

So the success of our catalogue campaign has really shown us a bigger lesson – that people are people, not just audiences, or users, or visitors, or data files, or anything else that we become tempted to talk about when we talk media. The medium is not your business . . . people are.

However excited you get about your online marketing strategy, remember that people need tangible reality too. Not instead of, but as well as. Something they can touch and feel, that feels 'right', will only enhance their trust in your brand.

DIRECT MAIL

How it works: This refers to anything that you send directly to customers in the post, from a catalogue to a postcard. It's easy this way to give customers a *call to action* – a discount or special offer using a promotional code or specific web address – which you can track and measure. This means you know how many people have responded to a particular piece of mail. There are other measuring methods available too, such as matching back postcodes to new customer addresses. Make sure you are working within data protection laws when it comes to capturing data about people's names and addresses, and also that you have a clear and easy way for people to unsubscribe should they no longer wish to receive anything from you.

Pros: It can be cost-effective, controlled and measurable, a good way of driving a large number of people to action. *Door drops* in particular are a cheaper method of distribution as they don't involve postage costs. You don't deliver to specific addresses but to postcodes that you have identified as being the most appropriate for your target audience.

Cons: Direct mail can be expensive, from design to printing, although these costs are negotiable. Postage, however, is not cheap and is non-negotiable.

RADIO ADVERTISING

How it works: Commercial radio stations sell advertising slots – and sometimes make the ads for you too. Ads need to be approved before airing. The airtime can be booked directly with radio stations.

Pros: Ads can be localised to be better targeted. You can book the times of day your audience is most likely to be listening. For example, if you need mums, you can target the school-run times. Radio is often listened to on or in conjunction with using the internet, so it can be a good way to advertise with an immediate call to action to the customer to find you online.

Cons: Even with careful targeting – choosing the right radio station and time slot – it's tricky to measure how successful an ad has been, unless you have a specific offer or competition for listeners, which can make you feel unclear about how well you've spent your money.

PRESS ADVERTISING

How it works: Ads in newspapers or magazines are sold according to their size, whether a small classified ad or a double-page spread. Right-hand pages are also more expensive than the left as they are more likely to be read – watch how you browse through a magazine next time you're waiting for the train. You can also buy advertorials, which are ads designed to look like editorials. You supply the copy in this case and the publication will produce something according to the brief. Any ad supplied must be in the exact format required by the magazine or newspaper.

PRESS ADS ARE STILL A VERY EFFECTIVE WAY TO ALIGN YOUR BRAND WITH A PUBLICATION.

Pros: Press ads are still a very effective way to align your brand with a publication – for example, fashion in *Grazia* or gadgets in *Stuff* magazine. You can be sure of reaching an audience that is definitely interested in a certain topic relevant to your business, whether health, pregnancy, food, interiors and so on. Most publications also have a website so you can buy paper and online advertising together.

Cons: It's a hard medium to measure, so you don't always know whether the money you've spent on the ad has translated into sales, unless you offer a discount or deal available only to readers.

Phew. All of that is a 'quick' guide to the things we wish we'd known when we started. There's no one answer for you when it comes to the best marketing channel for your business; you need to dip a toe into several of them. If you don't, you'll always be wondering what you're missing. And if something stops working for you, don't worry: you're not doing anything wrong, it's just that they all have a lifespan. Tweak, adjust and try again.

Remember: go slowly, surely and carefully. But go.

WE ASKED OUR PARTNERS...

How have you used marketing to boost your business?

Paul Warner, When I Was a Kid, traditional toys and gifts:
'I knew social media had potential for my business, but never knew quite how much. Now, 25 per cent of our annual turnover is generated through social channels. It can be fun, too, and a great way to build a rapport with customers.'

――――――― ? ―――――――

Betsy Benn, personalised prints and cards: 'Appearing on the front cover of a notonthehighstreet.com gift guide was an honour I imagined to be a once in a lifetime thing, so I was delighted to be given a second opportunity to design a personalised print for the catalogue. I didn't have to think twice about seizing the chance, and the print has continued to be a good seller. In all, we sold over 5,100 products last year, and had a total business turnover of nearly half a million.'

What is your best marketing tip?

Helen Lindley, Lindleywood, handmade wooden birdhouses:
'In the early days, when the orders aren't flooding in, invest time in getting to grips with PR, marketing and social networking to help get your business off the ground. But never stop learning – I'm now taking an SEO course to learn the "dark arts"!'

?

Emma Tucker, Modo Creative, personalised gifts and prints:
'Don't ignore the power of marketing and creating a strong brand identity. We invest as much money as we can afford in marketing, and constantly test and review what works to make sure we spend in the right places. You can't expect your business to keep growing without it.'

#6

MONEY, MONEY, MONEY

FACING THE FEAR AND EARNING IT ANYWAY

'Cash is king.'

Anonymous

As we hope we've made clear from the start, running your own business is about making money. Although other factors matter greatly – being in control, doing something you love, working with people you like – if you're not making money, then you are doing no more than funding a hobby.

But we also know that money can be a scary thing. Not just the pressing need for it to pay the bills, but the language that is often used around it. Cash flow, profit and loss, *fixed costs*, *capital depreciation*, venture capital, *equity* stake and other equally terrifying jargon bandied around by men in pinstripe suits seem designed to give us the jitters and prevent us from ever getting to grips with our own dough. Did you know that women are statistically more likely to get divorced in their lifetime than change their bank?

In this chapter, we want to demystify money for you. It's vital that you learn to get comfortable with the concept of making it, keeping it and managing it. Don't be coy about wanting your business to do well financially: it's the honest and decent thing to do for you and your family. And we'll give you the tools to understand the terms so that you can play those money men at their own game. We know how important this is because we've had to do it. But we also know it's important to separate personal finance skills from business finance skills in your mind. When it comes to personal finance, we're not very brilliant with money ourselves – neither of us has a trophy cabinet of ISAs, a pension portfolio, nor a record that is squeaky clean of overdrafts and credit card borrowings to help us along with ordinary life when we needed a bit extra. In the early Noughties, after all, most of us were doing the same – it's all that short-term debt that has made the recession such a deep one, and a global problem. If you've done it, you know you're not alone.

But when it came to business, it was a different matter – and so it should be for you, too. It can be for anyone. Business finance is another thing, and while being good at one often goes hand in hand with the other, there is absolutely no connection or reason why you can't tackle it afresh. Prior knowledge of SIPPS will simply not help you when you need to write a *cash flow forecast* or *P&L* (no, we didn't know what it meant either). Having got to grips with essential money language, we can now safely say in our meetings with our CFO or investors that we can talk their talk. We refuse to be befuddled by spreadsheets or blinded by mathematical science into signing up to a loan that causes us more harm than good. And yes, even our personal bank accounts have had an overhaul and we're no longer emptying the children's piggybanks to pay the gas bill. But it took blood on the walls for us to learn our lesson and we don't want that to happen to you.

OUR STORY...

We know what it's like to have no money at all. Less than no money. At one point in our business, a few months in, just when we were beginning to feel that we'd nailed this thing, we came within weeks of losing everything we had put into the business, and a lot more besides.

The thing we hadn't accounted for (pun intended) was that once you've started a business, it gets harder, not easier. The stress cranked up to boiling point – and we were feeling the heat. With our sellers on board, we had to deliver, bringing in the business we'd pledged to them. We were gaining staff, who depended on us, and – most of all – we couldn't let down our families, who had given both their money and trust. Winding up the business would have cost far more than just closing it down and going back to square one afresh. We had spent the bank loan, for starters. We didn't have the option of not keeping going, and we couldn't let ourselves down. We didn't just want this to work, we needed it to.

For the first six months and more since we'd launched, we'd been working fifteen-hour days as well as every weekend and we hadn't paid ourselves once. We barely saw our families, friends were some kind of distant concept in an address book and we'd forgotten what a hangover felt like (except that feeling that tired feels like a permanent hangover). At the same, we were ecstatically happy to be running our own business, we could really see the potential and lots of things went our way. Sellers were signing up, the site was getting thousands of visitors and we had landed some fantastic PR. Simply walking into our very own office was a joy in itself. But it was still hard work, harder than we had imagined it could be.

Despite working on a shoestring, the cash flow was sporadic. And this meant that when we were very tired, it was easy to lose perspective. And things kept going wrong. Expensive things. Highly unexpected things. At our lowest point, we took ourselves into the meeting room for a good cry and when we came out, our staff politely ignored our red-rimmed eyes.

We made a decision early on to be open and transparent with our team about how the business was doing. We shared the good and the bad, and when it was tough we brought them into that hell, too. (We just didn't particularly want them to see our tears.)

There were good times, because every day we were signing up more partners and visitors were returning to the site. But we hadn't anticipated that every time we grew as a company, we would have to accommodate that growth. With every new business we took on came the need to market more, acquire more customers and develop more features on the website. We already had the overheads of a bigger business, but since our main income was the commission we made on each sale, revenues were inevitably going to be small until we scaled up. After less than a year of operating, we needed to take on more staff to cope with the growth and allow us to match our potential, but our finances were in a parlous state. Without additional funding, the venture was in serious danger of imploding.

Yet we were turning business away. Even in dire straits, we knew we had to keep all the sellers and their products on the site at the high standard we had set. We wanted to establish in the minds of the British shopper that we were providing a way to shop that supported small businesses without compromising on quality. In our first year alone, we turned away £1 million of business from companies who applied to sell with us, but who were not in the 10 per cent we knew would succeed and deliver on the style and promise of the notonthehighstreet.com brand. If sticking to that promise only meant a few more months of not paying ourselves, then we knew it was the right thing to do.

But with our energies and minds turned to every other aspect of notonthehighstreet.com, we weren't keeping our eye on the *bottom line*. Around the summer of 2006, just a few months after we'd launched, alarm bells were beginning to ring. We didn't so much ignore them as feel pretty confident they would stop. The peals grew louder, but because we could see that we were doing well in other ways – visitor numbers to the site were increasing all the time, we were finding fantastic new partners who were signing up – we didn't react with the urgency that was required. Suddenly, in October, we hit a wall. It became apparent that if we didn't do something to bring in a massive life-saving injection of cash, our business dream was going to turn into a gruesome nightmare.

Holly: 'My grandmother died, which was a very sad time for the family. On the day of her funeral, I took a train with my father and it was only then, taking those hours out of the office, that we sat and took a proper look at the spreadsheets. Heart in mouth, we realised we were in real danger of losing everything we'd put in, and much, much more.'

These emails were sent to each other when we really felt we were on the brink of going bust . . .

From: Holly

Sent: 05 October 2006 14:36

To: Sophie

Subject: RE: have just put in £1,000. can't put any more yet and cheque due to go out of the same account

Ok – I have transferred 5k but it takes 7–10 days . . . .

AARGH, I cannot get hold of any more cash.

Plan??

From: Sophie

Sent: 05 October 2006 14:40

To: Holly

Subject: RE: have just put in £1,000. can't put any more yet and cheque due to go out of the same account

And I will have 5k on Weds but then will need to transfer. So basically again 7–10 days.

What's the minimum we need BEFORE then? Can maybe find another £1,000 . . . MAYBE. ONLY MAYBE.

Holly this feels like meltdown – we HAVE to laugh.

Sxxxx

We had just enough money to keep the business going until after Christmas, at which point we would have to shut it down. That was the real sting in the tail. We knew that we would see sales thrive over the festive holidays (and they did). But that wasn't going to be enough. Sophie's parents had made us one last loan, and Robert spelled out how many

PRACTICALLY ANYONE WE KNEW WITH MORE THAN A TENNER TO THEIR NAME GOT A PHONE CALL AND OUR BUSINESS PITCH RATTLED OFF TO THEM.

more cheques he could write, explaining that after that point he would have to draw a line as all his savings would be gone. The diagnosis looked fatal.

And yet . . .

As we geared up for Christmas, we called everybody. Practically anyone we knew with more than a tenner to their name got a phone call and our business pitch rattled off to them. At one point, we called Richard Branson's office and asked to speak to him (they said they'd take a message, but frankly we're not sure he ever got it). We told everyone we knew to ask everyone they knew if they knew anyone who might invest. We were operating on the basis that if we threw enough mud at the wall, something would stick.

There was an upside. As terrible as this was, it forced us into business maturity and some critical disciplines. We wouldn't recommend it as a path to getting organised, but seeking funds from a venture capitalist (one of the options we were investigating, of which, more below) meant we had to knock everything into shape, from our legal requirements to a monthly reporting system and the overall business model. It gave us, ultimately, a great grounding and added weight to the business.

We had a very near miss with one investor, on whom we pinned all our hopes and worked extra hard for weeks to secure the deal. On one horrible day, it all fell through: the day of shock and awe. We were too stunned even for emotion. It felt like a viciously cruel blow: to have been so close and done everything right and still to fail. We were just days from closing the deal when the axe fell. It wasn't our fault – the company that was backing us had hit its own problems. But that made us feel even worse, as if the gods were truly against us. We thought our time was really up and our lawyer started to talk us through some basic information about liquidation and receivership. We needed a miracle.

We got one. Sitting in church, our PR director Julie was chatting to a well-connected entrepreneur in the pew behind her. Did he know anyone who might invest? Actually, he said, I do. And that was how we met our saviour, Tom Teichman from Spark Ventures. Known as the man who wrote the first cheque for the founders of Lastminute.com, Tom was always looking for the next new idea – and he gave us a meeting. That fateful day, we made our pilgrimage up to town with our PowerPoint presentation and a huge bag full of samples of our partners' products, including personalised gifts for the Spark team and their children too. We knew we were presenting for our lives. It went well, we got on well, and

Happy days with Tom Teichman

our hour was up. Tom and his team thanked us, said goodbye, and left the room – they had another meeting to get to.

Our hearts sank. We silently packed up our samples, feeling a little foolish now, taking away our personalised t-shirts and customised door stops, folding them and packing them as hastily and with as much dignity as a scented floral bag of sand will allow. We knew what this meant. There was simply no more time left. Holly's dad, Robert, gave each of us a little smile. 'You did really well,' he said. We picked up our bags and made for the door.

There, in the corridor, was Tom. He beckoned us back into the room. 'I've just had a chat with the team,' he said. 'We're going to do it. We think you've got that spark. We'll speak tomorrow.' And he left again.

From up, to down, and straight back up again, we were breathless with emotion. But we had done it. We were on our way.

There was one more problem. By this point we were so close to running out of cash – we were getting into new debt just to pay off the older lot (which we are not proud of – don't do this at home, folks) – that even though Spark Ventures were keen, we didn't know if we could keep the company going long enough while we negotiated the terms and went through the extensive legal formalities. Having felt the elation of rescue, we were faced with the knowledge that we were minutes away from having to call it a day. In the middle of the storm, we had been thrown a lifeline and now we didn't know if we could reach it. Going through *due diligence* and contract negotiations was torture – on the brink of meltdown, we had to fastidiously produce market reports, references and financial *projections* for weeks and weeks.

Just in the nick of time, Spark came through, on Valentine's Day 2007, giving us an immediate chunk of funds, which was followed up early the next year with some more. In return, they gained a significant minority stake in the business and a place on the board. That deal enabled us to survive and grow until 2008, when we went out for another round of investment. The figures were getting bigger, which was good news, and exciting. But we had to learn a lot, and fast.

THE WORLD OF BUSINESS FINANCE

When you head out into the world with your idea, you need to face it with confidence. A huge part of that is understanding your business and your numbers. You need to know every part of your company inside and out so that you can talk it up in a way that investors will know and respect. There's possibly something of a male/female divide in this regard, and we wish there wasn't. Work with us to eradicate it. Typically, a woman will talk with feeling and conviction about her customer and what drives her, about her product, and why it's the best – that's a hugely valuable trait that men sometimes lack. But ask her to talk with the same fluency about her *top line* high season *run rate*, and her jaw will clamp firmly shut.

If you yourself are not a numbers person, then get someone who is and listen to them. You wouldn't try to fix a serious plumbing issue with a spot of DIY, would you? Get them rigorously looking at your figures. Allow the truth about money to give you a reality check – which is not to say that you shouldn't trust your educated guesses and have intelligent faith. The idea and the money should be brought together.

We know it doesn't look like much fun at first, but there is simply no point in trying to make a single sale, pitch a piece of PR or even write a detailed business plan before you have done a complete forecast.

Money dictates the terms of your business – what you can do and when you can do it – so listen to the numbers on the page: they are the urgent, unignorable facts you need to know.

TOP TIP

An accountant is a necessity, not a luxury. Even if you're someone who is good at maths, you need one. The only person who doesn't need to hire an accountant is an accountant. Find someone you like who is financially savvy – not necessarily chartered but trustworthy and experienced – and ask the questions, even the ones that make you feel like Miss Stupid of Stupid Land. The trust has to be absolute. They should be able to help you with your projections and may also be able to help you with a bank loan – some even have unofficial relationships with banks. They can also explain the intricacies of VAT, income tax and so on, which you must be aware of. It's impossible to run a business without an advisor. The range of types of accountants and cost is huge, so here are our tips on finding that person:

- Accountants can be expensive, so be selective. You're buying a service here. Typically, a better accountant, giving you valuable business advice, will be more expensive. Don't, of course, get one you can't afford.

- You might not need a chartered accountant yet – although having that qualification is a belt-and-braces assurance that they are the real deal.

- Get quotes upfront and negotiate a fixed fee if you can.

- Make sure they're good – for you. Sounds obvious, but don't assume they are. Do they have the relevant experience for your type of business? Can they answer your questions? Do you understand their answers?

- They should be able to support your business, not just fill in your tax return for you.
- If the accountancy services relate to your business, their costs can be tax deductible.

Know this, too: no one is too creative to understand a *balance sheet*. Or: you need to be a jack of all trades to run a business. We ask the creative people we work with to carry their share of responsibility for the bottom line.

Sophie: 'I'm less inclined than Holly to spend time poring over a spreadsheet. But good advice from a marketing agency creative director – and great friend – helped me to realise that commercial nous is not the exclusive preserve of an elite and numerate breed. That has given me the confidence I've needed to understand the money side of the business.'

THE TWO-YEAR PLAN

(and the skills you need to acquire in order to write it)

In order to understand your business and its finances, and to be sure it stands any chance of success, you need to create a set of spreadsheets that together will become your two-year plan. The dual elements central to this are your twenty-four-month profit and loss forecast (referred to as 'P&L'), and your twenty-four-month cash flow forecast. They are intrinsically linked, being two views of exactly the same information. The difference is that the one – the P&L – is about your ultimate profitability, and the other – the cash flow – is about whether you're going to have enough cash in the bank at any one time to get there. One day, you might add a balance sheet too, as part of this suite, but don't do that for now. And one word on this from our CFO: you need to do all the work in steps one, two, three, four and six below – but it's step five, the cash flow, that is your highest priority. Cash is king. Never forget it. The good news is that your accountant – or trusted financial advisor – will be able to help you with your two-year plan.

THE QUESTION OF A SALARY

There's another important reason to get to grips with P&L and cash flow: they will tell you what salary – if any – you can earn from your business.

Knowing your salary potential is highly motivating because earning your own money is not only significant in terms of the bills it pays – it is the best piece of evidence you can get that you are doing the right thing. One of our favourite stories is that of our partner Gina Axell, the founder of Rosiebull Designs, which makes embroidered textiles, such as personalised glasses cases. Gina launched the business, selling exclusively through notonthehighstreet.com, in April 2010. Within six months she was able to resign from her job in a primary school to work full-time from home. In her second Christmas, 2011, she earned more in one day than her annual salary as a teaching assistant.

In one way, deducing your salary should be quite simple. Sales less Costs = Profit.

From that figure, you can pay yourself. Ask yourself honestly: is that enough to live on? Do I need to reinvest in the company? Does it leave some for me? If not, back to square one. Are your costs too high or your prices too low?

But it can get more complicated. Profit does not necessarily mean you have cash in the bank – your customers have to pay you first and receipt of payment is not always immediate. This is what we will explain as the difference between cash flow and P&L. You also have to allow for the fact that if you have to buy stock or materials in advance of future sales, you will need to have enough cash to do that. You may also need any early profits to be reinvested into the business straightaway, so that you can buy any equipment needed as your company grows. You may have staff to pay – even if only part-time or seasonal. This may mean that all your profit cannot go towards your salary. This is why the cash flow forecast (as below) is so vital.

That said, you mustn't forget about a salary – it is ultimately the reason for your business. Even if you don't think you can pay yourself for a year or so, include a salary in your future costs and remember to include a pay rise as time goes on. The best way to pay a salary is as *dividends*, because they may be more tax efficient. Ask your accountant.

STEP ONE

Learn – or get access to – spreadsheet skills

Learn to use Excel or Numbers (if you can't already), including how to write formulas, or find someone who can do that for you, on a frequent and regular basis. It's just not possible nowadays to operate financially without that capacity. Even if you don't learn, being able to talk 'columns' (instead of 'the vertical lines'), 'rows' ('the horizontal lines') and formulas is vital. There are various online courses that teach spreadsheet skills, as well as evening classes – you won't have to do many to get to grips. Or ask a nice friend who can teach you. Learning to get comfortable with a spreadsheet is worth its weight in the gold your business could earn.

STEP TWO

Establish what your costs are

The question we are most frequently asked is: 'How much money do you need to start a business?' The answer: whatever you think you need, then double it. Then double it again.

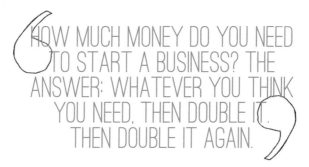

HOW MUCH MONEY DO YOU NEED TO START A BUSINESS? THE ANSWER: WHATEVER YOU THINK YOU NEED, THEN DOUBLE IT. THEN DOUBLE IT AGAIN.

Here's a brief list of costs to think about:

Set-up costs

We're just asking you at this stage to think about what you might have to spend your money on. Later we'll tell you how to organise these figures.

- Decent writing paper with your letterhead on it (important for formal business correspondence, such as to your bank, lawyer or accountant).

- Branded presentation material (when you pitch the business – whether for a contract, to introduce yourself to a new customer, or to win investment or PR – you will want good-looking folders, printed information, possibly a PowerPoint presentation and so on).

- Legal work (e.g. trademark registration).

- Setting up as a company (accountant's fees and company registration costs, although when you start a business you can be a *sole trader*, which is more cost-effective initially).

- Office equipment (new phone line, printer, computer).

- Staff recruitment (if necessary).

- Space from which to run your business even before you make your first sale (even if this is at home, you may need storage items and/ or a desk).

- Website.

- IT (such as new wiring, or help with setting up a computer network and email accounts).

Ongoing costs

- Rent, fuel, utilities.
- Payroll (salaries).
- Employees' benefits (if anyone works for you then you also need to pay their holidays).
- Total cost of goods you are selling (raw material, postage).
- Equipment or machinery.
- Professional services (lawyer, accountant).
- Subscriptions/memberships (e.g. for publications to keep you up to speed with your business sector).
- Marketing activity and material (including on and offline advertising and PR).

Holly: 'Anywhere we could save cash at the start, we did it. If an ink cartridge was running low, we'd take it out, give it a good shake and get another few days' worth of printing before forking out for a new one. We still keep a very close watch on every penny. We cancelled an ad recently even though it was only a few hundred pounds because it couldn't be justified.'

STEP THREE

Establish what your revenues are

What are you selling and how much money is it going to make you? Be it a product or a service, how much of it can you sell and how often? This is called your top line income – simply, the money coming in through the door. Be confident and knowledgeable about your pricing. We talk to our partners a lot about pricing for profit – there's no point in being modest here. Indeed, sometimes underpricing can lead to worse sales, not better. Research your market thoroughly to understand what is a competitive price, and make use of what you already know about costs to give you an initial sensible figure that you can work with as you move to the next stage.

HOW TO PRICE FOR PROFIT

This is a critical area and one which many of our partners struggle to get right. The problem is that often when you start a business, you're so eager and grateful to any customers that you would almost give your things away if it meant they were happy. But prices are hard to change – at least, your customers don't mind if they go down, but they certainly notice if they go up – so you need to get them right first time around. Your prices need not only to cover your costs, but also to make your sold product a profitable one. In other words: the right price means you get a salary.

To get it right, you need to think of all those costs in a different way. We talk about costs quite a bit in this chapter, but the areas you need to make sure you have included for this purpose are:

- *Hidden costs*. These can be tricky to identify initially, but if you don't include them in your calculations you may get caught out in the future when you expand and have to start paying for something that was previously free. For example, those few hours of help someone in your family gives you in return for tea and biscuits. The internet or telephone bills you currently pay for in your household direct debits. Anything your business couldn't function without needs to be identified and included.

- *Sales volumes*. As your sales volumes increase, you may benefit from *economies of scale* where you can improve on the price you are paying for materials. Not just discounts for bulk orders, but also reaching the *VAT threshold* means you will be able to claim back VAT paid on materials, services and commission.

- Future costs. Think of costs you may have to incur in the future if your business grows as you hope it might. This is a challenge, but you need to think ahead as much as possible because it may be difficult to radically change your prices at a later date without directly impacting on sales. These things might include: staff, rent, materials, stationery, bank fees, marketing, delivery, photography, couriers, travel . . .

(In case any of this sounds familiar, it does cover some of the same items in Step Two but is a different view of it.)

Next you need to look at three different ways of pricing. Try them all out and compare them, to see which will work best for you.

Bottom-up pricing (or, covering your costs)

Split your costs into fixed (those that don't change, no matter how much you sell) and variable (those that change according to your sales levels, such as materials and postage). You should end up with two figures: say

£1,500 a year in fixed costs and £17 as the cost of making one handmade silk cushion. Then consider how many items you think you can sell in a year. To do this, estimate how many you can sell in a week, but don't multiply by fifty-two weeks. You need some time off! If you have any kind of sales history, that will help you to forecast.

Divide your fixed costs by the number of items you think you can sell in a year and add the *variable costs* of making one item to this to create a base price. Remember that certain elements of your costs, such as VAT and commission, may vary depending on the price point you select, so you may need to adjust your final price up or down to take this into account.

Top-down pricing (or, what you think customers will pay)

Consider what you think most customers would be happy to pay for your item. To do this, you want to think about the target market for your product, where they shop already, how much *disposable income* they have and, therefore, how much they might be willing to pay for your product.

Another key thing to focus on is looking at similar products in the marketplace and how prices compare. Quality is pivotal – if you believe the quality of your product is superior you can adjust your pricing to reflect this, although you need to be careful not to price yourself out of the market. You may need a lower price point if you are starting out, to encourage customers to give you a try. But that lower price point should still be making you a profit. Be mindful that in order for it to make sense for your customer if you later decide to raise your prices, you may need to change your product in some way too, even if the real cost to you hasn't changed much.

Sales-based pricing (or, dreaming of how big your business could be)

If you're not sure of the sales potential of your product or service, do you have a sales target for the year? Whether that's turnover or how much profit you know you need to make, whether supplementing a main income or having to cover all your living expenses. Consider the value of your time and how you would feel if, after all your hard work, you made £500 this year, or £5,000, and the impact that could have on your lifestyle.

Take that sales target and divide by the number of items you think you can sell in a year.

Result

At the end of all these calculations, you should have a range of results that look something like this . . .

To cover your costs you need to charge a minimum of, say, £23 a cushion. To be competitive and offer value for money for your target customer, you can charge anywhere between £20 and £85. To achieve your sales goal for your company, you should charge £33.33 per item.

You can then use these methods to finally decide on your price point, confident that you have considered all angles and set your product price at a level that works for your business. Once you have worked through an individual product's pricing, it's worth reviewing your range, if you have one, to ensure it features a spread of price points. This will enable you to appeal to as broad a range of customers as possible.

N.B. For customer clarity, we recommend that pricing follows a consistent format – for instance, we always suggest partners round to the nearest 25 pence. Pricing randomly across your range at, say, £1.97, £2.43 and £4.00 will look unprofessional.

STEP FOUR

The profit and loss forecast

A P&L is a financial statement that sums up the revenues, costs and expenses that are incurred over a specific period of time. You need to create a two-year P&L, broken down month by month. With this record in hand you will have the information you need to show the ability of your company to generate profit by increasing revenue and reducing costs.

Now's the time to start putting your spreadsheet skills into practice. We'll leave you – or your Excel-friendly friend – to work out where you need to write formulas, but in short, you need to put the months of the year across the columns at the top, with totals for a year at the end of each twelve months. It does not, of course, have to start in January. Then down the side, write the headings and fill in the numbers along each row. Note: we're assuming that you are not registered for VAT at this stage, but see 'A brief word on . . . VAT and tax on profit' on page 198 for more on that.

In your P&L forecast, you now need to arrange the costs you thought about earlier – set-up and ongoing costs – in these spreadsheet rows:

- **Sales income figures.** Make conservative assumptions about the sales you will make over the two years. Show these revenues (income) exclusive of VAT, because that money is really just passing through your till to go straight to HMRC. Do include any discounts you plan to give (for example, a summer sale).
- **Direct costs.** These are the costs that are directly related to a sale. So that would include the actual cost of raw materials, and other costs involved in making your products, and any other cost that is incurred in making a sale, such as postage charges. To be clear – don't show this as lump sum costs incurred in building up your stock (this cost will sit in your cash flow forecast, below). Costs for marketing your business don't go here either. Think of it this way: direct costs will vary based on the sales you make. If there are no sales, the costs will sit in your unsold stock.
- **Overhead costs.** These are costs that you pay regardless of your monthly revenues from sales. Staff salaries (including your own), rent and office costs (including printing ink, paper but not equipment – see the next item), storage costs, marketing, legal and accounting costs, software and so on. These are your fixed costs. Even if you don't make a single sale, you will still have to pay these costs, certainly in the short term. (Sometimes in the longer term, if you have a rental lease for an office.)
- **Capital costs.** This is where you account for the money you've

spent on office equipment or machinery needed to run your business. But don't show the lump sum total here. Instead, what you show for these in the P&L is the average rate of depreciation of the asset (i.e. how much value it loses each month – think of it like a car, worth less as each month goes by), which is spread over a number of years. The use of the equipment will normally cover a longer period than your P&L so, in other words, if you need a new computer every three years, then divide the cost of one by thirty-six months and put that monthly cost in across the twenty-four months of your P&L.

N.B. Costs should include VAT if you are not registered for VAT.

You'll need a 'totals' row below all that to show the results of those pluses (income) and minuses (costs), for each month, and then the totals for each year. That's your profit or loss before tax. And after that, some more rows will be needed to show the effect of tax.

So the lower part of your spreadsheet will look like this:

- **Profit or loss before tax:** After taking into account all your income and costs, you then arrive at either a profit or loss before tax. Profit will incur *corporation tax* if you are a limited company. If you are a sole trader those profits will be included as self-employment income in your income tax return.

- **Tax:** Then add a line to show your expected tax – this is where you definitely need an accountant to help you.

Which brings you to:

- **Profit or loss after tax:** Your final and important total. What is left over after all these costs and taxes have been deducted is your *net profit*, which you can either take as bonus income for yourself or reinvest back into the business. (Either pop the champagne cork here or put the bottle back in the fridge.)

A brief word on...

VAT AND TAX ON PROFIT

VAT:

- You're unlikely to need to register for VAT in the earliest days of your business.
- There is a new level set each year as the income allowed before a company must register for VAT. You must check each year what that is.
- It's vital that a small business registers for VAT when it reaches the set level. There are severe penalties for 'forgetting' or 'not realising you had to'.
- Unfortunately, as soon as you register for VAT, you have to charge that to your customers, and that means adding (currently) 20 per cent to your product price. This is less of a problem if you are selling to other businesses, because if they are registered for VAT, they can offset it just like you will be able to on your costs. But for a non-business customer, that's a real price increase.

- However, registering does also mean that if you pay VAT on buying something, you can offset that against the VAT you pass on to the HMRC. That means your outgoings should be less costly for you.

- How VAT works is that you are effectively handling that money on behalf of the HMRC, taking it for them and then passing it on, less any VAT you've already paid on outgoings.

- VAT payment to HMRC normally happens quarterly. Your accountant can help you with that.

- Never miss a VAT deadline. However, there are a number of schemes that HMRC offers to make it a little simpler to track and pay. See their website for more information.

Tax on profit could be:

- Corporation tax: This is only payable if you are a limited company, making a profit.

- Income tax: This is what you pay if you're a sole trader or partnership.

On either tax, if you make a loss in your first year, but a profit in your second, you can offset (deduct) the loss from the first year so that you pay less tax in the second year.

STEP FIVE

The cash flow forecast

This is what everything is building towards. You need to know if the money is going to hold out. Remember: cash is your ruling master. The difference between the P&L and the cash flow is that the cash flow demonstrates timing, allowing you to see at a stroke how much money you will have at any given moment. Having done your P&L forecast, the twenty-four-month cash flow forecast comes next. This will translate your P&L into a statement of cash coming in and costs going out, taking into account the timing of those receipts and payments.

This cash flow breakdown will also show if your company needs to borrow any money or raise investment capital, how much you need, when you need it and how you will repay any loan. With a forecast that covers two years, you should be able to see ultimately if you can make the business a viable proposition. Crucially, it helps you identify how much you need to raise to set up your business. It's more than just planning ahead: it shows whether you can survive while you grow a bigger business – or not.

Start a new spreadsheet. Across the top write the next twenty-four months, month by month, plus columns for totals at the end of each twelve months.

Down the side, head up one section as 'Cash In', with three subheadings. The figures need to be put in across the months:

- **Investment.** Any capital (lump sum) investment in the business – how much money you or others will permanently put into the business at the beginning or later on.
- **Loans.** Whether bank loans or temporary financing from others. Show the lump sum or sums going in at the time you will receive them.

- **Sales.** Revenues coming from sales you make to your customers, taking into account any credit terms you give them (if, say, you allow payment to be made in instalments).

For the next section below – 'Cash Out' – write down the following subheadings:

- **Direct costs.** These are the same costs you put into your P&L, but this time spread out over the months at the times you will actually be forking out for those materials.
- **Overhead costs.** These are also the same costs you included in your P&L, spread out over the months, and here you have to make sure you take into account the credit terms you have negotiated as well as the timing of the payments. For example, if your rent is normally paid quarterly in advance, that will look different on your cash flow than it does on your P&L.
- **Capital costs.** These are also the same as in your P&L. Show the full upfront costs of buying any machinery and equipment. Do not show monthly depreciation. This is just your shopping bill at the time of purchase.
- **Loan repayments.** The monthly sum you need to pay on any loans you have taken out.
- **VAT and tax on profit.** The payments you will need to make to HMRC, if you are registered, and any other taxes.
- **Set-up costs.** As we've said before, these are the initial costs to start your business. This could be purchase of equipment,

manufacturing or buying your initial stock, legal and accounting costs. These costs will also appear in your overheads, but as the costs for ongoing advice. This should be a one-time cost as you set up your business prior to starting to trade.

Your bottom line on this spreadsheet will show the cash you have coming in, minus the cash going out. If it is positive, it will allow you the opportunity to use the cash to reinvest, pay back loans, and so on. If it is negative by more than any overdraft facility you have, it will give you the clear picture that you need to find new sources of cash or even go back to your business model again – although your P&L is the better test of your overall business model. If your business is seasonal, it will allow you to see when the negative cash occurs and alert you to providing short-term solutions (such as a bank overdraft).

Profit generated over time by your business on your P&L should be the same as the positive cash flow. If it isn't, that's simply a case of your maths not adding up. Remember, the P&L and cash flow are two ways of looking at exactly the same raw numbers. Over longer periods of time, the totals should synchronise, and if they don't, you need to go back – with your financial advisor, whether friend or pro – and check where the figures are going wrong.

We know this long-term planning can be difficult, and many are often daunted by having to put it down on paper. But if you don't do it, you could run into serious trouble too far down the line to get yourself out of it. Don't kid yourself that you can short-cut on this exercise.

Once you've done your two-year plan and cash flow forecast, then you can get down to business (assuming the numbers have added up in your favour). This brings with it a whole new set of skill requirements and jargon. Keep bearing with us. It's not a doddle, but it is doable.

STEP SIX

Record results

Keep good records so you know all along how profitable you are. Each month, check your actual figures against your forecast and your cash flow – that's a discipline you have to get into. In other words, are you tracking correctly against your two-year forecast, or is the reality very different? Produce a spreadsheet of your results and note your cash balance at the bottom. If things look very different from what you planned, you'll need to re-forecast. Don't wait for the accountant to come along and prepare your annual accounts and then announce you made a loss or, worse, for the bank manager to tell you you've exceeded your overdraft. There is a lot of cheap software, such as Sage, on the market to allow you to monitor how profitable the company is on a regular basis.

THE NEXT MOST IMPORTANT BIT: FUNDING

It's very likely that in the early years you will not make a profit, so you will need to find some sort of funding for those losses. Furthermore, you need to think long-term about your cash requirements. Look three to five years ahead and think about ways in which you might fund expansion. Below are some of the funding options available, how they work and their pros and cons.

BANK BUSINESS LOAN

How it works: The bank lends you money, with repayment over a set number of years at a particular interest rate. A business loan is usually personally secured against your assets – both personal and business – although *unsecured loans* (e.g. a loan that does not put your home at risk) are slowly making a comeback. We strongly urge you not to set a loan against your home, even though banks may try to persuade you to.

How much can you get? Most banks offer between £1,000 and £25,000. You can find some willing to go beyond £100,000 depending on the security and business prospects you can offer.

Pros: Reliable and secure, you are assured the money for the duration of the loan. The odds of a bank or major lender requiring payback in one lump is tiny, so long as you keep up with repayments. Compared to other forms of finance at this level, a bank loan is reasonable in cost. They're not cheap, but they don't carry the interest rates or charges of credit cards and overdrafts, and they don't ask you for a share of the business.

Cons: The terms and conditions of a loan are very tight. Borrowing more than you need means you will fork out needlessly for extra interest. If the loan is secured against your home or other assets, they will be at risk if you cannot afford to keep up repayments. *Secured loans* usually have lower interest rates, but you must be careful to ensure you can afford repayments. There can be other costs such as an arrangement fee or charge if you repay early.

GOVERNMENT GRANT

How it works: Neither a loan nor an investment, a government grant is a sum of money given to an individual or business for a specific project or purpose. Finding the right grant for you and your idea can be akin to searching for a small penny very far down the back of a vastly oversized sofa. There are several bodies that provide business grants, including – but not limited to – the EC, UK central and local government, bodies such as Regional Development Agencies, Chambers of Commerce and County Enterprise Boards. Grants from these sources provide support financially, as well as giving access to expert advice and services.

How much can you get? Most government grants require you to match the funds you are being awarded (whether you match them personally, or from retained profits, a loan or another investor), so you

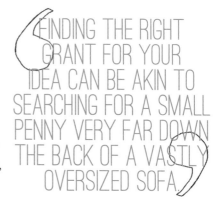

FINDING THE RIGHT GRANT FOR YOUR IDEA CAN BE AKIN TO SEARCHING FOR A SMALL PENNY VERY FAR DOWN THE BACK OF A VASTLY OVERSIZED SOFA.

won't get the whole amount you need. You also have to demonstrate that your business is able to fund its share of the total costs. The amounts given vary from grant to grant.

Pros: You won't have to pay the grant back (the government considers that it makes the money back in the form of taxes they are paid when the business is successful and profitable). Nor do you surrender any equity in the business.

Cons: The eligibility criteria are very stringent and can depend upon the location, size and industry sector of the business. Even with these narrow criteria, competition is very strong. Grants are also usually only given to proposed projects, not ones which have already started, which could leave you hanging for a while. If you do not follow the very strict terms and conditions, immediate repayment of the whole grant may be required. We know that very few of our partners have secured grants: out of the 1,826 we put the question to, just ninety-one received a grant somewhere along the line. The amounts available rarely warrant the work involved, and it is often too complicated to find one that is relevant – something we think the government should fix, urgently.

MONEY FROM FRIENDS AND FAMILY

How it works: If your business needs immediate and relatively short-term funds, it may make sense to approach someone you know for a loan. If the business needs longer-term or permanent funding, then you may want to consider giving your investor a share in the business. Borrowing from a friend or someone in your family can be a way to get money fast. But there are emotional implications, taking the riskiness of this kind of funding into a realm of its own.

How much can you get? It depends on their largesse. But whether a loan or an investment, no one should lend or invest more than they can afford to lose.

Pros: Generally, someone you know will offer flexible terms. The loan may be offered without security and be interest-free or at a low rate. They may also agree to a longer repayment period or lower return on their investment than formal lenders. On a personal level, if they know you and your circumstances well they are less likely to ask for a detailed business plan (though you should have one anyway).

Cons: If you pay interest on the loan, there will be tax implications for you both. You also have to manage their expectations carefully – make sure they understand that the money they invest is *risk capital*. In other words, there is a risk they won't get it back. Equally, if all goes well, they may look for returns that reflect that risk – greater interest than they would have received if they had left that sum in the bank. You need to be sure that both of you are absolutely crystal clear on the terms of the arrangement. Any misunderstandings can damage relationships. Those close to you may risk more than they can afford to lose, or they may need to ask for their money back at a time that doesn't suit your business. They may want to get more involved in the business than you feel is appropriate. Think twice about approaching a friend or family member if other sources of cash have turned you down – there may be a good reason for it. If your business fails, investors lose their money. That will be on your conscience.

Holly: 'When I first borrowed money from my dad to start up Your Local Fair, as an accountant, he knew a lot. So not only was he completely inside my business plan, but he was very strict in terms of a repayment plan, although I used to renegotiate terms with him every year over a few glasses of wine at Christmas. I eventually repaid him in 2011. As my dad and advisor, he could always see that I was matching funds and he knew what I needed. The same happened when we were looking for funds for notonthehighstreet.com, but we eventually turned those loans into shares in the business. The main thing he did for me was help pay my childcare fees in those early days. That's still on my tab.'

VENTURE CAPITAL AND BUSINESS ANGEL INVESTMENT

How it works: Selling shares in your company is one way of raising long-term finance for your business (this is also known as *equity finance*). Shares in a company represent ownership – so when an individual buys shares in a company, they become one of the owners of the business. This entitles them to a share of the distributable profits (or dividends) of the company, if there are any. Shares issued by a small business are usually done in return for a lump sum investment – at this level, it's got nothing to do with stock markets. *Business angels* are wealthy individuals who invest in high-growth businesses in return for equity (a share of the ownership). Some angels invest on their own, others as part of a network, syndicate or investment club. They are often experienced entrepreneurs themselves and so can bring their own expertise and contacts to the company, as well as money. On the whole, venture capital firms – companies that exist solely to find the right businesses to invest in – look to invest larger sums of money than business angels in return for greater equity.

How much can you get? Anything from tens of thousands to millions of pounds. Each investor will have their own view of what sums are large enough to provide a good return.

Pros: Investors only get the return they want if the business does well, so they are on your side when it comes to running and growing your start-up. As it's not a loan, you won't have the ongoing repayment issues, which means any capital you have can be kept for business activities or reinvestment. Investors of this nature expect the business to deliver value, so they will work to help you explore and execute growth ideas. If you have a good match with an investor, they will bring invaluable skills, contacts and experience to your business and may even help with strategy and key decision-making. Many investors will be prepared to offer follow-up funding as the business grows.

Cons: Raising this kind of finance takes a huge amount of time and energy, and can take your focus away from your core business at a time when it is in a fragile stage. Potential investors will seek comprehensive information on you, your background and the business – this is called due diligence. They will look at past results and forecasts and may interview your management team, if you have one. Depending on the deal you strike, you may lose some of your autonomous power to make decisions about the company. The deal can be highly complicated, involving negotiations around types of shares, voting rights and *exit* plans. As the partnership is ongoing, you will have to make sure you set aside time to provide regular information for the investor to monitor. You will have a reduced share in your own business (although if it wouldn't have grown without the investment then you'll make more money in the long run). There can be quite complicated legal and regulatory issues to comply with when raising the money. Your investors will eventually want to sell or exit, and that in itself is a responsibility and concern for you to manage.

Sophie: 'Taking capital investment is all about timing. It's a huge asset for a business to take on capital funding but, in general, the earlier you accept it, the more of your business you have to give away in return. So weigh up whether the time is right.'

TOP TIP

Anyone who invests with you will always want to feel that you are looking after their money and that you understand the significance of their investment. So even if you're not asked, always produce monthly accounts that show you are on top of your finances, together with a monthly summary of your business. This should cover all the key aspects of the company (see KPIs in Chapter 3) and include a note of any issues you have had and any opportunity you are exploring. Always be respectful in your dealings with your investor (even, or perhaps especially, if it's your dad/sister/best friend's husband) and if you have to make a large financial commitment, ask their opinion. If you work with a bank or VC you will have to do this as this will be in your agreement anyway. In sum: treat people who have helped you with respect. Remember – you might need to go back for more.

PERSONAL BORROWING

How it works: The easiest, cheapest way to provide your own financing for your new business is to use your own savings. But this can be risky and you may not have enough to cover all the funding you need. There is another option, which is called personal borrowing – getting a mortgage (or second mortgage), personal loan or borrowing on credit cards – but we recommend that ideally you don't do any of those. If financing your business has come to this, then you've got to be as sure as hell your business is going to succeed. It's one thing to put in your savings; it's quite another to get into debt that could lead you into murky waters.

If you feel that this is the route you must take, then we urge you to think very, very carefully before borrowing any amount of money in this way and always to aim to match the financing exactly to your needs. Do not over-extend yourself. You should also leave a contingency fund, in case you need it to see you through a difficult period.

How much can you get? An unsecured personal loan from a high street bank tends to be capped at £25,000. Most new credit cards don't allow for more than £2,000 on spending, if that. A mortgage depends on the value of your home and the amount you can afford to repay each month. Obviously, you must be clear to the lender about how the money will be used.

Pros: Paying for your business yourself gives you far more control than all the other options – you're not giving away any equity, nor are you vulnerable to an outside investor or lender withdrawing their support suddenly. You remain personally in control of your borrowing.

Cons: Repaying credit card expenditure over a long time is very expensive. Some loans can be inflexible – you may end up paying interest over several years. If your business fails, your home and any other assets could be at risk. Knowing how much you've borrowed at a personal level can put a lot of pressure on you and your family.

SOMETHING ELSE FINANCIAL YOU NEED TO GET COSY WITH

Once you get into the realms of big money, there are certain tricks of the financial trade that are acceptable practice and buy you a little time when you most need it, although they can carry a cost. Sometimes, for example, it is necessary to delay payment because your cash flow demands it. Ways of doing this include:

- Delaying payment to *creditors*. You must get their permission first. Keep communicating – agree a payment plan and stick to it. If you have any further problems, you must call them, otherwise they may decide to go down an aggressive route to recover their money – whether that's a debt-collection agency or the small claims court.

- Selling on debt. If you're having cash problems because you're owed money, companies will give you the cash and chase it up to keep for themselves – for a price.

- Making sure your customer pays. Make it a habit always to track invoices you've sent out and watch that the money is coming in. Don't be too polite about reminding people what they owe you. If someone places a very big order with you, it is advisable to run a credit check on them first.

LAST BUT NOT LEAST: DEBTS AND LOSSES

Going out and raising money for notonthehighstreet.com forced us to grow up very fast. Neither of us has ever been rich and, although we had been used to handling large sums of money on behalf of former clients and employers, needing and holding what seemed like untold fortunes for our own business and the businesses we were servicing was a very different beast indeed.

The word 'debt' for example, in a personal context, can be very frightening, particularly at the extreme end, with its implications of loan sharks, inordinately high interest rates or small print that says 'your home may be at risk'. Even when debt is less scary than this, it was the nation's collective credit card and mortgage debt that sent us tumbling into the recession. So you're right to be wary.

But in a business context, debt is something else. We have come to think of it less as debt and more as a point in time. There will be financial dips in your business across the calendar year and when debt happens then, it is simply a part of the journey, so long as you know where you're going and keep checking regularly. Unnecessary fear of debt holds many back (but keep a good hold of the necessary fear!).

In business, there are also losses. It's OK to make a loss. Many companies famously made losses for years – Amazon, Twitter, Facebook. You do, however, have to scale that back to be relevant to you and the size of your company, and there does have to be profit in the forecast. Sometimes, when every penny you make is being reinvested into the company, the idea of real profit can feel hopelessly far away. But so long as there is a path to profit, you're doing well.

Don't be afraid of money. It's there to work for you.

WE ASKED OUR PARTNERS...

What's your best money-saving tip?

Mat Brown and Laura Marlowe, The Orchard, vintage-inspired garden and home wares: 'Don't scrimp on the secure packaging of products. Although it may cost you a little extra at first, you will save so much money in the long run. It took us a while to realise that the time and money it was taking to sort out damages caused in transit far outweighed the initial cost to the business.'

?

David Emery, The Drifting Bear Co., bespoke prints: 'Put all the money you owe the tax man into a high-interest savings account and leave it there until you need to pay it. It keeps you from spending it and also builds up some interest.'

?

Vicki Smith, sgt smith, children's fashion: 'I wish I had employed an accountant from the start – it would have saved us a lot of money in the long term. I would then have set up the business as a limited company from day one. It may seem like a big leap to incorporate a company on a new idea, working out of your spare room, but it does help you to focus and see your business as a separate entity.'

?

Jayne Bradshaw, Swings & Pretty Things, home accessories and gifts: 'Never order at a trade show – go home and look at the product again. It is so easy to get carried away with the excitement of it all and then panic when you see the size of the order!'

What do you enjoy most about the financial side of running your own business?

Gina Axell, Rosiebull Designs, embroidered textiles: 'That I can pay someone else to do it! I'm not brilliant with the finances, but my accountant is a family friend who has taken the time to explain things to me so that I actually do feel as if I understand what is going on. That in itself is quite satisfying.'

— ? —

Stefan Boehm, Goose Bedding, natural luxury beddings: 'That you are in total control of where the business goes and how you are set up to achieve those financial goals. Also, you can see where every aspect of spending goes and what is and isn't essential, and where you can make savings without compromising your values or quality.'

— ? —

Rachael Rower, Grace & Favour Home, textile home decorations: 'Knowing exactly what is working and what isn't, and being able to adjust accordingly – being small means I can implement changes almost instantly, and make instant savings.'

— ? —

Hazel Morrison, Hazey Designs, silver and gemstone jewellery: 'As sad as it sounds, I love filling in my accounts book every time I make a sale and seeing how big the book is growing.'

What was the biggest financial mistake you learned from?

Lucy Uren and Graeme Purdy, Rowen and Wren, modern interiors: 'As with many new businesses, we started on a tight budget. But we learnt very early on that it doesn't always pay to cut corners on costs. In particular, we learnt that if you're going to spend money on anything, it should be the presentation of your products. If they are well presented, they will sell themselves and potentially provide free marketing, which is invaluable.'

?

Ashley Todd, Ella James, vintage-inspired wedding and home accessories: 'Paying too much for a PR company to promote our products in the first year. We found it difficult to cover the extra cost and the benefits were negligible.'

?

Andrew Dennison, coconutgrass, graphic prints and artwork: 'I was a little over-enthused and caught up in the buzz of raising my brand awareness. I decided to buy some flyers to promote my products, but put one too many zeros on the end! We've got enough wrapping paper now to last us a lifetime.'

?

Lucy Lee, Lily Charmed, silver charm jewellery: 'Security! When setting up my working-from-home office, I spent more on the colour of the walls than I did on security. Big mistake! We were burgled in August 2011, a few weeks after launching, then again on New Year's Eve. We lost stock, computers (and two months of work) and our sanity. Now we have a safe, an alarm and a 'cloud' back-up system for our documents.'

When did you first pay yourself a regular salary?

50 per cent said they still don't pay themselves – they either reinvest the money or take money only when they need it.

20 per cent paid themselves for the first time after twenty-four months.

15 per cent between twelve and twenty-four months.

5 per cent between six and twelve months.

10 per cent in the first six months.

How involved are you with the finances of your business?

5 per cent said a close friend/family member does it for them.

45 per cent said they do it all themselves, including tax returns.

50 per cent said they pay an accountant to do it.

Do you have contingency or emergency savings?

50 per cent said no.

#7

(THE NON-EXISTENCE OF)

WORK-LIFE BALANCE

*'For fast-acting relief,
try slowing down.'*

Lily Tomlin

Broadly speaking, there are two types of people who dream of starting and running their own business. Those who believe they have a fantastic idea and the wherewithal to make it a success. And those who don't want to work for someone else – those who want to escape the rat race and be their own boss. The latter quite often believe that this path means choosing your own hours and therefore improving your work–life balance. Hmm.

How this phrase ever even came into being is a mystery to us. Few people we know would claim to have a work–life balance. Most of us are just trying to get everything done, without thinking about any kind of philosophy behind it. And how's this for irony: the week we had to write this chapter, we were at full-stretch working on a major new deal for notonthehighstreet.com; one of us dropped an enormous bowl of bolognese on the (newly laid) kitchen floor and it smashed spectacularly, leaving the walls and ceiling looking as if a massacre had taken place; we heard that a close family member is very ill; and we were staging our first ever AGM. We ended up squeezing out the words in between board meetings and helping with homework.

Whilst ultimately we've learned to cope with stress, we won't pretend we don't suffer with it at times. What we do know is that it's an inevitable part of life and it can be a driving force for good, when the adrenaline powers you on to achieve. But you have to find your own personal decompression toolkit, otherwise you'll burn out.

Sophie: 'Don't call it "time management", call it "getting things done". I get up at 5.45am so that I can have a couple of domestic hours, sorting out the laundry, walking and feeding the pets, getting everyone up and ready for school. I also use this time to stem the flow of work emails before I hit the office. If there's an hour to get something done, then do it.'

But if you asked us what is the toughest thing that women have to deal with when they set up a business, it's lack of time. The time starvation reaches new levels and doesn't have the compensations implied by that delightful – and wrong – expression, 'Cash rich, time poor'. You're time-poor not least because you're cash-poor. It feels so acute, the time shortage, that it almost hurts. You need to be three people at once and with no money to spare you can't buy the rescue packs that other businesswomen operating at that kind of intensity have access to (e.g. PAs, domestic help and mobile beauty therapists). Being the caring, sharing sex, knowing you can't be there for the people who need you, can induce severe guilt.

One thing we know for sure: running your own business is not the answer to an easier life. While we are a bit more in control now than when we worked for a boss, we can't say we particularly feel it. We certainly don't work fewer hours. There are lots of reasons for setting up your own stall, but spending less time at the office shouldn't be one of them. That said, we're with Malcolm Forbes ('No one ever died wishing they'd spent more time at the office'), and our solution is to make your time at work pleasurable. We're not saying it isn't hard work, but that hard work can be a good thing.

Holly: 'I think I speak for our partners and us when I say that if you set up your own business it's because you either love the industry, the product you create or find, or the change you make to others. It's certainly true for me. I feel I was born to do this. I love the products we sell and admire the talented people who have come up with them. My job is my hobby, and my hobby takes up most of my waking hours. So being interrupted on holiday, at night or over the weekend is far less painful than it sounds. Especially when it gets me out of the washing up!'

Having worked since we left school, neither of us has ever known anything other than a more or less constant catch-up struggle in our lives, to stay on top of work, enjoy our relationships and give time to our families. Pursuing our own interests has always taken a backseat. In many ways, our work is our interest. We don't mean that in a geeky workaholic way – 'Jeez, but I just lo-o-ve accounting!' We mean that, for starters, we love looking for beautiful things. It was a real revelation when we realised that something we liked doing could be work. And while the fun of looking for nice things doesn't occupy much of our working hours anymore, we do genuinely get a kick out of growing the business with clever and brilliant people alongside us. We're learning all the time and that, for us, is a real boost.

That said, we get tired, overwhelmed and emotional now and then. We're not going to lie. When you're ambitious, starting a new business – and then growing it, as we are with notonthehighstreet.com – is a full-time thing. Not just physically but mentally. While we agree with the view that workaholics throw hours at a crisis rather than trying to come up with time-effective solutions, there are going to be occasions when you have to pull an all-nighter to meet an urgent deadline. And of course we agree that you shouldn't go to bed late night after night – being knackered never did anyone any favours. It makes you cranky, unfocused and stubborn. But you'll find that even when you do go to bed, you're awake half the night, your 'to do' lists churning around and around in your mind. Sometimes it's just easier to get up at 5am and start work. We can't predict how it's going to be for you – you'll just have to suck it and see. And it doesn't last forever. If you make a success of it (and if you follow what we say, you've got a good chance of doing that), then payback time will be a comfortable house, good holidays, nice food to eat and a decent glass of wine when you get home.

Sophie: 'In the beginning, I think I got through it by saying to myself, "It's just one last push – this is the last week/last month, and then I won't have to work until 3am." And eventually it came true. There was a time when I worked every Saturday. That felt miserable – worse than

Mondays. I'd feel cheated, as if the whole world was getting up to start the weekend and I had to get back to work. But it got better, it really did.'

HOLIDAYS AND DOWNTIME

We once read that everyone should aim to have a fortnight's holiday every three months. Which sounds ridiculous – who can afford that much time off? Or that many holidays, for that matter? – until you realise that it was decreed by a female CEO, a woman who holds one of the world's most globally important jobs (just 8 per cent of them are held by women). That holiday time is her secret weapon that means she can stand the pace – it's her survival kit.

We've never achieved the same kind of holiday time, but we do use that as a benchmark to aspire to. We know that women have a tendency to avoid holidays out of some kind of guilt and then, when they do go, they spend the whole time worrying about what's going on back at the office. But downtime is essential.

Holly: 'For the first few years, there weren't any real holidays. If I did take a week's break, I'd be so exhausted I'd just sleep throughout the entire thing. As the years went by, I realised I was becoming hooked on the adrenaline rush – the pace and excitement of work became hard to live without. In the beginning, I knew that the business was missing me and that felt very stressful, knowing that I couldn't take even two weeks off without it taking months of planning and worry. Now I know that everything is very well managed without me and the problem is me missing the business. Only after two very different holidays have I finally worked out the solution.

'A few years ago I had the best holiday of my life. I went to Australia for three weeks and it kick-started our international expansion. I met lawyers out there, I had meetings. Not only did I feed my habit, but I came back to the office refreshed and brought something massive back to the company.

'One year later, I went to a resort – five-star hotel, white sand beach, the works. It was an enormous privilege to be there and I felt . . . pretty miserable on the whole. I ended up at the bar, chatting with someone, the two of us confessing that we were having a tough time being away from work. Neither of us could admit to anyone else that we had sunk into a depression in the middle of paradise.

'Being on holiday in a remote place with no internet and patchy mobile phone reception was like being a heroin addict going cold turkey. I couldn't cope. And it was made worse by the knowledge that I should be having the time of my life, teaching my son how to swim in turquoise waters.

'Anyone who works the hours we do has to have time to recover. But now I know that if I combine a holiday with work, I'll have a good time. I've already lined up some meetings for my next trip – to Canada. It's going to be wonderful.'

You probably won't have a holiday for a few years, or at least until you have staff who can do what you do. But don't put it off for any longer than you have to. Any business has a downtime period – that's your time to go away! Don't forget long weekends if you can't manage an entire fortnight. Plus, when building a business, you can come to an agreement with yourself, as it were. Go on holiday, but accept that you will spend some time checking emails. (But be strict about limiting it – for everyone's sake – unless an issue comes up that absolutely has to be dealt with there and then.)

HOLLY'S MASTERCLASS ON HOW TO COPE WITH HOLIDAY HELL

(not including cockroaches in the bathroom)

- If you have booked a holiday, you will either have taken steps to make sure things can run without you for that time, or you know already that you have the staff in place to manage things. Trust in them. Leave them to get on with it. (One man we know didn't have a mobile phone for years because, he said, when he'd had one he would come out of a long meeting to hear seven messages. The first would say: 'Boss, can you call us? We need your help on something.' This would be repeated with increasing urgency, until the last message, which would say: 'Don't worry – we've sorted it.' In short: if you're not there, they'll probably find a way.)

- Equally, you know that it's almost impossible nowadays to be truly out of contact for more than a few hours. They'll get you if they really need you. And if there's a chance you'll be needed, don't take that trip to the middle of the Gobi Desert just yet.

- Buy several business books at the airport. Write notes from them and take the best of the advice back to the office with you on your return. (Doing this gives me the hit I need, and then I'll be smiling quite genuinely for the next few hours.)
- Tell whoever you're going on holiday with that if you're going to be relaxed, you need to get your fix and they must please try to understand. But promise to set limits: an hour of emails in the morning, an hour of phone calls in the early evening. No more.
- Remind yourself frequently that taking a break from work is good for work. You need to be as disciplined in your downtime as you are in your 'on' time.

While neither of us has a hobby, we do find ways to switch off. We didn't learn the lesson in the early years – and we wouldn't have had the time even if we did – but we know now that taking time to recharge is essential to our performance as businesswomen.

Sophie: 'I'm rubbish about holidays. I'd probably never go on them if my husband didn't mind so much, but thanks to his organisation we have had some very happy family ones where he coaxes me out of my stress and soothes me with cocktails. My personal priority is to take time at home to stop and slow down. If I've been feeling particularly overwhelmed, then I take a couple of days at home just to potter about, clean the fridge and get back to baseline.'

STAYING HEALTHY

When we first started the business we all put on weight – we called it 'the notonthehighstreet.com stone'. We were just too exhausted, too mentally occupied, to think about exercise or watching what we ate. Regular rounds of chocolate biscuits and birthday cake were frankly what kept us going through the long hours. Any time off was too precious to spend alone in a gym when we could be with our family or sofa instead. But after the first three years, we realised we had to turn this around. We really passionately believe that you have to look after yourself because your business is sure as hell not going to look after you. If you let your business dictate your health, it's the quickest route to being unfit, fat, wrinkly and ill.

Sophie: 'I do quite a lot of exercise now, and I'm pretty rigorous about it. Twice a week in the gym and one run of about forty minutes. Believe me, I'm no Jessica Ennis, but it makes the difference for me between fit and unfit, sane and insane. Everything you hear about endorphins is true. That's why I do my run at the weekend, partly because of the adrenaline withdrawal. I take Rufus the dog for a run. We bond. My spirits lift and I come back. All is right with my world and I can merrily get started on the businesses of a family weekend.'

It's true: time and money spent on staying fit and healthy is an investment in you and your business. If you still need persuading, we asked a personal trainer, Tim Hagon, for the three physical and psychological benefits of exercise on your working life:

- Increased energy. The body was designed to move – hence a lack of movement, sitting down all day, is a killer. You need movement to keep your brain working at full capacity, to keep your limbs limber (no exercise can mean they stiffen, causing pain). Only moderate exercise is needed: a brisk walk can increase your energy levels and decrease tension.

- Increased self-belief and confidence. Overcoming physical challenges that you didn't think were possible will improve your muscles, respiratory system and make you feel even better about yourself. Results don't come easily – you're not going to feel good about yourself if you sit on an exercise bike reading a magazine. Train hard and the chances are you will want to work harder.

- Increased positive attitude. Exercise has been shown to beat stress and anxiety, as well as sharpen intellect. Other people will pick up on your positive energy and will therefore be more inclined towards your way of thinking, improving your powers of persuasion and leadership.

STAYING SANE

There are three cornerstones in anyone's life: yourself, your family and friends, and your work. With hindsight, we have realised that at any one time you will only manage to give time to two out of these three things. Those may alternate – sometimes your family will get neglected, other times your work, more usually it's your own self. But rather than suffer the indignity of a losing battle, learn to accept that one thing at a time will have to be sidelined.

Holly: 'For the first couple of years of the business, I didn't properly understand that I couldn't give everything to everything. I failed to compartmentalise things in my mind and piled them all into one big mess. This ended up making me quite depressed. Looking back, I wish I'd known then not to get so hung up on my weaknesses. Some of them turned out to be my strengths. If I hadn't recognised that I wasn't so good at the details when it comes to running a business, for example, I wouldn't have partnered up with Sophie. It's only because we work together that notonthehighstreet.com is the success that it is. So ultimately, my flaw turned out to be an asset. When you're working for yourself, you do have to be a jack of all trades at the start, but you can sort it out and delegate as you move further along with your plans. When you work for someone else, you have to be a great all-rounder as you would never dare tell a boss that you couldn't manage a particular task. Try not to over-compensate for the things you can't do and think positively about the strengths you do have.'

Much like the 'quality quota' we've mentioned elsewhere in the book, when it comes to your home life you've got to mark out those things that you need to get absolutely right, others where you can live with OK, and apportion your time accordingly. If you can live without the bathroom being cleaned for a week or daily hoovering, then don't pressure yourself to get it done more frequently. Likewise, if you absolutely have to have ironed shirts, then spend Sunday night getting a week's worth pressed and hung. Be realistic about what matters to you – forget about anyone else's opinion on whether it matters that you don't get your husband presents for your wedding anniversary or that the car is filthy – and prioritise in a way that suits you, without shame.

Sophie: 'My home is my haven of calm. I'm under a lot of pressure from my children to stop being such a control freak – I can't bear it if their rooms are messy or there's dog hair all over the armchair – but I can deal with it because I know it's my retreat. I can't apologise or give it up any more than anyone else could give up their haven.'

The other key to sanity is to stop procrastinating – again, as much as at work, you should practise this in life. Stop feeling the guilt, just do it. Stop trying to make everything right, just get it done. Don't let things pile up or they will overwhelm and flatten you.

- When you've got an urgent task to complete, switch off email and the internet until you've done it.
- Write lists. (More on this below.) These really help.

- Limit yourself to five principal tasks a day – any more than that and you won't achieve them. Only move on to the rest of the 'to do' list once they are completed.
- Dare we say it? Be more like a man. Don't fret, do.
- Be OK with what's OK, live without what you can live without (even if others can't), make time for what matters.

How Holly stays ahead

Holly: 'In everybody's day there is thinking time available. You need to find yours. Even if it's your fifteen-minute shower or your commute into work. For the last few years, I've disciplined myself to take an hour to walk to work every morning. Knowing I have that daily hour has enabled me to be consistently effective and to achieve my goals.

'On the walk, my laptop is in my rucksack, my phone is on silent in my pocket. I use the fresh air to clear the cobwebs and first of all I go through my 'to do' list for the day, in my mind.

'Once I've done that, I start to think about the rest of the month or year, and what's going to be happening at the end of it. Then I'll take two or three things that have been planned for the year – perhaps goals that have been set or actual events in the diary – and focus on those in the walk.

'Mentally, I'll work through each thing, planning every step. On each landing area, I'll imagine telling someone else about it, explaining what's happening, how I got there and where I'm going with it next. This means that when it comes to actually discussing those things, I've thought it through to the point where it feels as if I've done it already. This not only helps me feel in control, it enables me to work out what is doable and what isn't, and gives me the confidence I need to talk it out with someone else.'

FRIENDS

For everyone, friends are hugely important. We know you know that. But it's a harsh truth, for us anyway, that when something's got to give, it's time with friends. The tough thing for us at the beginning was that, for our friends, our life with the business was new to them. As they weren't going through the same thing, they would say, 'Well, if you can't make tonight, what about tomorrow?' and we would want to reply – and sometimes we did, and regretted it – 'What makes you think tomorrow is going to be any different? Or next week? Or next month, for that matter?' Invitations to family holidays and girly weekends would make us weep. It made us, ultimately, a bit jumpy and defensive. Did they think we were just sitting on our backsides, getting rich? We knew they didn't, not really, but we felt on the back foot, just the same.

We were always afraid our friends might have believed we were busy – too busy to see them – because we were having an amazing time being successful. Or did they think we had changed and were no longer interested in going to their birthday party or meeting up for a regular cup of coffee on a Friday morning like we used to? It couldn't have been further from the truth.

And we knew they, too, were full-on and stressed and worn out from the many demands of their own lives. But we also knew that 'one glass of wine' on a Wednesday night would flatline the rest of the week, and we could never afford the time we'd lose. We had to explain to our friends that we weren't trying to cut them out of our lives, but that our monthly dinners had to become three-monthly instead.

It does get better. People get used to the 'new' you. They can see that you haven't changed, your circumstances have. Our friends are good ones, and good people, so they're on our side. Though there were a few near misses that could have ended very sadly. The important thing is that they didn't. The hours we keep are still erratic and we're still horribly unreliable – which we hate – but we and our friends are used to it and we have all made our peace with it. Luckily for us, most of our friends have been supportive, lovely and understanding, letting us know that they will still be there for us when we eventually get back to them. And there is more time for them now – it's not anything like as bad as it was.

Holly: 'I had a very low point when my best friend of thirteen years called me up and told me what a bad friend I had been. And it was true. It didn't matter that she didn't know what it was to have a new baby at the same time as trying to run a company that was, at that time, looking as if it might fail. Her situation was one of life and death – someone close to her was extremely seriously ill – and I was not there. It killed me. It was alien to me not to be there for the people I cared for and yet I had nothing else to give. I was run dry – everything I had was either given to Harry, then in the first year of his life, or to my second child, notonthehighstreet.com. I can hardly talk about what happened between my friend and me to this day as I feel such shame. Looking back, I fully understand what happened and while I can never forget, I have forgiven myself. Fortunately, so has she – she has just asked me to be godmother to her first child.'

Sophie: 'I've been very fortunate. When I hit some terrible times – when my dad was very ill, or when the stress was getting to Simon and me – my friends were there for me in a trice. And yet I've had to make some very tough calls. Social life is out at times, and that's been my sacrifice. It couldn't be my husband, children, home or family. I hope I haven't neglected friends who've really needed me – you should be able to tell the difference between someone wanting a laugh and someone sending out an SOS. And I try hard always to remember birthdays and send thank you cards. In a funny sort of way, it's been wonderful to realise that even when I've deserted my social life, my friends haven't deserted me.

'As you get older, more and more of your friends will get tied up in their own busy lives and it's nice to know that at that point everyone understands each other. Of my friends now, one is the sole breadwinner of a family of five; one is a businesswoman setting up a big venture on her own (I can see what's coming for her); one is running two or three businesses and is the perfect corporate wife and mother too; another is self-employed and takes on crazy challenges such as cycling across

South America; and yet another is in a couple where they both work long hours but have three very young children and she's a semi-professional athlete, doing all the training that requires. So I think I'm lucky that many are in the same boat. We see each other just enough and bump into each other in the street sometimes, embracing each other like lost lovers, because the affection is still there, but we know that now is not the time for idle socialising. Just the same though, it will be lovely when that time comes . . .'

MARRIAGE/LOVE LIFE

It's a rare business that doesn't take its toll on a marriage or romantic partnership. We know that many of our sellers work with their husbands and, quite honestly, we don't know how they do it.

Sophie: 'Simon and I were never a textbook couple and we always did things the wrong way round – we didn't even get married until the children were five and three years old. But those first two years of notonthehighstreet.com were a big shock, and it just hit us like a train. We both were taken aback by the realisation of just how hard I was going to have to work. It

‘IT'S A RARE BUSINESS THAT DOESN'T TAKE ITS TOLL ON A MARRIAGE OR ROMANTIC PARTNERSHIP.’

took years of adjustment. Simon has a pretty intense career of his own, working in the City. On top of that, starting a new business means you're so exhausted, you're bad company when you eventually do get home.

'But there were good things too. Simon was excited about the business and the prospect of me being the main breadwinner and he always, always believed in me, Holly and the business. If anything, from my point of view, my husband is a central part of the company's success. He takes care of my state of mind because he is wise and level-headed. He soothes my anxieties, doesn't panic. He was also relatively relaxed because we had a game plan and that made some sense of the early years of chaos. During the second year of the business, it took its toll on our daily lives, but recently it's beginning to feel like all that effort is paying off. We've worked to get somewhere and now we've got somewhere.'

Neither of us, it has to be said, is much good at being the wife at home anyway. Being able to look our husbands in the eye and match them matters – we work just as hard, we bring in the same money. It means that you can dictate your own terms and can't be pushed around or belittled as previous generations were. That brings true equality to your partnership.

Holly: 'If I hadn't had the support of Frank in those early years, notonthehighstreet.com wouldn't be here. Simple as that. A couple of years ago he gave up work to become a house-husband – he's going back now – because we agreed that my career was possibly going to pay better dividends in the long run. We divided and conquered. But there's no

question that the whole process took its toll on the relationship, and I had
to remind myself to talk about more than work when I was with Frank.
In the earlier years of the business, we would have a date night, sitting
around our kitchen table with a nice selection of tapas and some wine, and
chat through the week to catch up. We tried desperately to give ourselves
time to be just us. We could let our hair down a bit and I think that time
kept us sane.

'We also tried to have family or friends over for supper every week,
and still do. It's so important to us to have them near us and share in their
lives. It keeps me in touch with the real world and with other people and
their concerns. It has been difficult, but after ten years together we are
finally coming to terms with the fact our world turned upside down for
a while. We're getting back to the old Frank and Holly and I'm looking
forward to things getting better.'

CRACKBERRIES

It's hardly news that there's been a massive culture change in the way we
use the technology around us since we first set up in 2006. The difference
in how we work compared even to ten years ago is enormous. We're all
still trying to keep up with the gear changes. The hardest to learn to live
with is the meshing of personal and professional communication: most
of us have one phone number and one email address on which we can be
reached by our colleagues, boss, best friend, mum and the plumber. Social
networking sites are a one-stop shop for anyone and everyone to come by

and say either, 'Hello, do you fancy coming out for a glass of wine?' or to make a comment about how the company is doing. Of course there is an off button for all this, but we're all too twitchy or too occupied to push it. Every now and again we'll be sitting on the sofa watching a movie, thinking how pleasant it is, and just as we glance down at our BlackBerry to check a message, we look sideways at our companions to see everyone's bowed heads lit by the soft glow of their electronic devices. Technology has taken over.

Sophie: 'I do try to switch the email off on my phone. There are times when someone in my family says, "You just haven't heard a word I've said, have you?" and goes off in a huff. But we're all on iPhones or iPads or whatever. It's not just me.'

Rather than fight this, better to adapt, we say. Set your own rules. When working from home it's tempting never to switch the laptop off and still to be checking emails or website analytics as you're watching the ten o'clock news.

The problems usually start if you fail to set yourself proper working hours. Rather than telling yourself that you have until 6pm sharp to achieve the tasks on your list, you tell yourself you have until midnight, thereby fooling yourself into believing that you have hours to spare. This takes the urgency out of the 'to do' list and leaves you vulnerable to one of the many enticing distractions available.

You may, for example, tell yourself that you're reading the news to stay abreast of current affairs . . . but find yourself straying onto the dailymail.co.uk's 'sidebar of shame'; or that you're on Facebook to update the company page . . . only somehow to find yourself looking at the photo albums of a school friend you haven't seen for fifteen years; or checking the blog of someone in the same business as you . . . then exploring the archives, just so you can delay logging out.

Set limits – and stick to them.

Holly: 'I'm very grateful that I can check my emails as they pop up on my mobile phone. It allows me to feel that I'm still dealing with things, while getting on with others. It means I never have that moment where I switch on my computer and there are sixty emails all requiring my immediate attention. But I do need to get better still at controlling its effect on my family life. I remember once, when my son Harry was two years old, he was desperately trying to keep my attention and he just pushed the phone away from me, staring at me. I've never forgotten that. Or, more recently, he was trying to talk to me and we kept being interrupted with alerts from various devices. We now have a rule that phones, iPads and computers are on silent if we are in the house together.'

A brief word on...

GUILT

There's a certain paradox to guilt, in that we have both now just about learnt not to feel guilty about the things we cannot change (time with our friends and family), but it's probably guilt as much as anything that ties us to our mobile phones and email. If one of us is having some downtime, then we worry the other is killing themselves to make it happen. Is the board emailing and not getting through? Will we look like a shirker if we don't reply until Monday? Is there a technical fault with the site of which we are in blissful and shameful ignorance?

There's no solution. Live with it or get over it.

SOPHIE'S MASTERCLASS IN LIST-MAKING

For work: When I first started at notonthehighstreet.com, I would have two A4 pages of 'to dos' for the following day. One or two bullet points that had not been achieved would get transferred to the next. But I would never leave the building until the next day's list had been written.

Now I have a red Moleskine notebook – more commonly used as a diary – which has the days of the week on the left and lined paper on the right. I'm very strict. On the left I write the things that must happen that day in each of the day slots. On the right, I write the things that must happen that week. I really try to discipline myself to keeping one list for the week, otherwise you spend your life re-writing each day what you didn't do yesterday, which is bad practice for lots of reasons.

When I'm not in the office, I'll email myself from my iPhone with things that spring to mind that I must add to my list or just do. My husband and I talk every morning when I'm on my way to work (he leaves the house at 5.30am and I leave at 7.30am) and often it's the only conversation we'll have all day. Sometimes I'll ask him if he could email me the list I've been storing up in my mind as I've been racing to get myself/the children/the dogs sorted and out the door. It somehow seems to help our bizarrely condensed relationship that we speak like this so I might as well combine it with planning my day. Bless him, he doesn't mind. Also, he sometimes says that he can do one or other of the things, so it doesn't have to go on my list.

When I get to work, I transfer everything I've emailed myself the night before and that Simon has sent to me that morning into my red notebook. Then I read my list and try to get a few things done and off it. I also sit down with my PA every morning, and she gallantly takes everything she can off me.

For non-work: While all this is going on, I have a list on my iPhone Notes app, for just personal stuff. Four lists, actually, that I constantly add or delete things from.

- **House:** As I write this, we're in the twentieth month of a seemingly never-ending refurb – we're down to hanging pictures now.
- **Urgent/this weekend:** This list is for things such as buying a birthday present, coffee with a friend, have a pedicure (this last

one never seems to get crossed off . . .). Every Sunday night I do a check on this list and if anything hasn't been done I ask my sainted husband to do it if it's truly urgent, otherwise it rolls over to the next weekend. Not quite like the lottery rollover, but still . . .

- **General 'to do':** This is all the non-urgent family/domestic matters. I write down absolutely everything, otherwise I just won't remember. Even when a button falls off a jacket, I put it on the list. Then, when I have a bit of time, like a few days off – hah! – I work through as much as I can.
- **Buy:** Clearly my favourite list. It currently reads: Red Diane Von Furstenberg dress (I will most likely never get it, but I love it), clippy things to stop mops and brooms falling over, giant mirror, picture frames for Ollie's room.

Every Saturday morning, I handwrite a list of the most important – or nicest – things on all those lists and start delegating. Everyone in the family gets their own list of things to do. It's a mixture of them being sweet and wanting to help, needing to get themselves organised, and taking the pressure off me. I do it in big writing on a big sheet of paper and leave it on the kitchen table. I also list out the work I have to do that weekend. If I can get through half of that set of lists, I'm doing well. At the end of the weekend, I have the joy of crossing the things off the four lists on my iPhone Notes app.

Enough.

PAUSING FOR BREATH

For anybody starting off a business, the beginning is always going to be tough on yourself, your family and your marriage. Time is consumed faster than a chocolate milkshake by a greedy child, your mind is constantly distracted by the business and it's hard to find spare energy for anything else. But that doesn't last. Nor does the stress go away. It's more that it shape-shifts. You will get to a point where you have fewer problems – but they're bigger problems. The important thing is that you find a way to make peace with it. Running and growing a business will be a huge part of your life – better to accept that than fight it.

Coach yourself at each stage to readdress different areas. Is your salary at the right level? Do you still need to work at the weekend? Is it vital that you get to work for 7am every day? Have you got the right amount of time in the year for holidays? You always need to review, to give yourself a breather. We can see the dangers when people work flat out for six years and forget to stop and look at the bigger picture. In those years, a practical situation may change – whether that's a different house, the children getting older or the business moving on to another level. You need to see whether that new picture is giving you new opportunities that you're otherwise missing out on. We take that time out ourselves – three days at the beginning of the year, out of the office, just the two of us, checking our ship is on the right course. That way, we hope we've got a good chance of heading into the sunset.

WE ASKED OUR PARTNERS...

Who is the most important person to your business other than you?

Claudette Worters, murano glass jewellery: 'My partner is a graphic designer and he does all of the photography of my jewellery for notonthehighstreet.com. He also does any graphics work that I need done, i.e. business cards, comp slips, packaging etc. But as we have two boys aged five and two years old, work and child care is a constant juggling act and I would find things a lot harder to manage without the help of my mother-in-law and my childminder.'

?

Heather Fox, Silver Kitsune, silver and gold jewellery: 'My dad, as he charms the socks off the ladies in the post office for me.'

?

Jo Norman, Daisyley, paper gifts and decorations: 'My two boys. They have constant faith in my abilities (ignorance is bliss!), telling their teachers and anyone about my business. They are proud of me and that is a wonderful confidence boost on days when things are not going well. I'm doing this for them so that we can all benefit from the extra money and the fact that I work at home. They suffer during the holidays and weekends because I can't 'go and play' until I've done my orders, but they never complain.'

Pipany Philp, Pipany, embroidered gifts and home decorations: 'My partner, Dave, has been the best sounding board as he is creative in thought but highly practical too. He listens and offers his advice when asked, without necessarily expecting me to follow it! He also is so supportive of what I do in terms of childcare when it is manic, such as at Christmas, and will turn his hands to cutting out, sewing or packaging if I am really stuck, as will all the children! My local post office is also fantastic and allows me to drop bags of orders off to be processed by them through the day, rather than me standing in queues and wasting valuable working hours.'

#8

LIVING HAPPILY EVER AFTER

THE TRUTH ABOUT BEING WORKING PARENTS

'We've begun to raise daughters more like sons... but few have the courage to raise our sons like our daughters.'

Gloria Steinem

As any working parent knows, the balance between the pros and cons of time spent in the office away from home is never evenly weighted. We had better warn you now that if you're coming to this chapter looking for the answer – we haven't got it. But what we do know is that even without a rock-solid solution, trying to make it work is worth it.

You may labour because you love it, but you will also do it because it's what keeps your family afloat: the roof above your heads, the meals on the table. Yet it's your business that can keep you away from said roof and table. There will be times when your children are proud of what you do and others when they hate it, for keeping you from them, for distracting you. Equally, there will be times when you resent having to rush back from a project that is going well to take over from the childminder or wonder if you can't have just one single day when your paperwork isn't pulled out and shredded/scrawled on/turned upside down.

In Britain today, 66.5 per cent of mothers work, 29 per cent of them full-time, and we think they're all amazing. There's no infrastructure in place to help them – these days, far fewer have grannies on tap – and childcare is eye-wateringly expensive, stretching any working family to the absolute limit. In our Afterword, coming up next, we write about what we think should be done about this. But in the meantime, we have to find our own ways to manage the situation as best we can.

If you run your business as cleverly and carefully as humanly possible – including following the practical guidance in the rest of the book – it can help you to plan your day and your working life well, heading off some of life's biggest stresses, such as finding yourself struggling alone with a hideous deadline or a cash crisis. All of which will have the greatest knock on effect when you get home.

If you're a mum (or even a dad), particularly one who has decided to start a business from home partly so as to have more flexibility around your working hours and your family, then we can't tell you how it is going to work out for you. Nor would we presume to give you advice on what childcare is right for you – that's a personal choice for every parent. We can only tell you what it was like for us. As being a working mum is such a personal thing, we can't even write this particular bit of the book jointly, so we're going to tell you how it was – is – individually. We hope it helps.

HOLLY'S STORY

When I was a little girl, I wanted to be a nursery teacher when I grew up. I loved children and worked as a babysitter from the age of fourteen, was an au pair in France when I was sixteen and was always the girl that you would find helping mothers at parties with their babies. It was second nature to me. But I was also impatient to start work, and when I realised I would have to study for years to qualify for a career with children, I decided that it would be better to work at something else and just have lots of children or even adopt them, so that I could still be surrounded by them.

When I had been with Frank for a year, we decided to try for a baby. We were lucky and in the end did not spend long thinking about the fact that we would be living on a policeman's wage, in a one-bedroom flat, and that I wouldn't have any money coming in! When I put on my last of the Your Local Fairs, I was eight months pregnant. Somehow we managed to get our first house just before Harry was born.

As I was still quite young myself, twenty-eight years old at the time, I only knew one other person in my entire social circle who had a baby, and she was six years older than me. I felt quite alone with my newborn as Frank had to go back to work two weeks in, and I knew the money was running out rapidly. I gave myself ten weeks' 'maternity leave' and I do remember trying to enjoy every single one of them. I still look back on those days with a huge smile. But I knew that we only had so many mortgage payments left in the bank. So when the time was up I just quietly got back to work as a freelance ad sales consultant.

At first, I had a nanny for half days – it allowed me to immerse myself in work for those hours and get used to handing my baby over. Mostly, I was very lucky with the nannies I hired. I conducted countless interviews, but the winning candidate always shone brighter than the rest.

Then, when Harry was six months old, I got a call from Frank telling me I was not to panic but he would not be coming home that night and did not know when he would be back. It was 7 July 2005 and Frank had been called to Russell Square, tasked with body recovery after the terrorist attacks on London. I remember turning on the TV with this little person in my arms and watching the news unfold. I heard from Frank now and then over the next six days, when he came up for air. He was driven back one afternoon with an escort waiting outside while he held Harry for one hour. We all sat in silence and just cuddled and shed tears. He soaked up enough energy and was whisked back to carry on dealing with something no human should have to experience. It hit us both hard in different ways. I didn't leave the house for four days and I know it has affected Frank deep down ever since.

After that, a sense of grabbing things with both hands seemed very right. I decided that I couldn't give up on my idea of working with the small businesses and now I needed to give it life. This was the summer I got in touch with Sophie. Harry was tiny, yes, but life was short and he needed two strong parents.

Working with Sophie and building up to the launch of notonthehighstreet.com was palpably exciting. I often call the business my second child and I am as ambitious for it, as driven for it to succeed, as any mother is. But it took me away from home and I struggled to come to terms with the fact that I wasn't there for Harry as much as I would have liked to have been. I suffered huge, massive guilt. I missed Harry's first steps – I cried a lot about that. Because his bed times were so early

Frank and me in love with our new baby, Harry

and I had to be out early in the morning, I could easily go four or five days without seeing him. Sometimes I felt as if I couldn't breathe. There seemed to be no chance to stop, but I carried the pressure of everyone depending on me to make the business a success. There was no other way but to carry on. My entire family's livelihood depended on me making it work.

Not only that, I wanted to be a businesswoman. I was trying to do both things – run the business and be a mum – completely, and it's just not possible. What makes it better, what eases the pain, are two things: learning to manage your own expectations and good childcare, whether that's a nanny, au pair, childminder or nursery.

In the winter of 2005 I got my second nanny, Kasia, for full-time work, and she was a godsend. Frank worked very long hours and we were never sure when he might get home. I was working all the time, too, but would have to be back for 5.30pm to let her go as she studied in the evenings. That was hard: to have to be somewhere at a specific time when I could rarely rely on anything to run on time at work. I know I drove too fast, too often, to get home, opening the door panting. We had a book where we worked out to the half hour how much she was owed each week. These were our hardest days financially, and I remember bursting into tears more than once when I realised I didn't have enough to pay her. She was so good to us, gave Harry such love and care, that I knew he was not affected by my absence in the day. I would always take him to doctor's appointments, even if it meant having to get home for just half an hour. These were things I felt I needed to do in order to be a 'good mother'. But it took it out of me.

Those very early years were the toughest. When it came to someone being able to compromise in order to manage Harry, it was always me. But because it was my own business didn't mean it was easier – if anything, at times, it was harder. I was trying to do too much: keep the house going, make sure the nanny had her objectives for the day set, get to work, work, try to get home on time, think about how to get food in and how we would all get fed. Every single night I'd have to think on my feet. I had no back up. My mum would come and help when she could, but she lives an hour-and-a-half away. That's no good when Harry had to be dropped off at the nursery, I had to get to work and the nanny had called in sick or arrived late.

On top of everything else, the business was in its infancy too, and that was gruelling. I had no idea what we had let ourselves in for and doing all that as a first-time mum with a young baby, trying to keep the roof over our heads as well as maintain my relationship, was punishing. I felt alone, even though Frank, my family and my friends were the most supportive they could have been. Not once did they judge me or utter the words that made me feel I'd let anyone down if I failed – of course they would rally around if I did, but they never even went there. They only had hugs, emails and texts of encouragement. Sophie, too, really helped me at this time, as a mother herself, pointing out that I may have missed Harry's first steps but so did lots of mums and he wouldn't remember whether I had been there or not anyway. Making a success of the business during his early years will mean that, when he's older, I can be there cheering him on at his sports matches and he'll be aware of that.

As Harry started to get older and turned into the loving, funny chap he is, I allowed myself to believe that I had not damaged him and that we had survived the worst. When at last we were able to pay ourselves and take a holiday or two, the better it was for our little family. What's more, I saw the company reach its potential and I knew it had been the right thing to do by him.

After Kasia left, we had another wonderful nanny – Lilly – but she eventually had to leave us, too. Each time it was as if a family member had died. Your childminder, nanny or nursery becomes the backbone to your life, making everything else achievable. Knowing that your child is happy and safe frees you up to do your work. I remember sitting in my car after hearing the news, in floods of tears.

After Lilly, we hired a nanny who was so terrible she only lasted seven days. Frank and I decided that we needed more consistent childcare and could not risk another mistake. So we took the decision that Frank would leave his twenty-two-year career with the police to look after Harry. In many ways it was a good plan, but much, much harder to live with than either of us anticipated.

Frank found it difficult to get used to days of looking after a 5-year-old, doing the school run, the never-ending washloads, dry-cleaning to pick up and homework to get done. We anticipated that the biggest change would be for him but I had a huge shock, too. I lost the right-hand women that I had always had in my nannies for five years. It took away my ability to run the house, to decide if Harry was well enough to go to school, to make sure there were enough vegetables on his plate and how the house looked. This shift in our roles put enormous pressure on our relationship. Of course we were both very aware of what a privileged pressure this was: Frank and Harry were so fortunate to have these years together. Few fathers can do that. But after two years of being at home, Frank is returning to work, setting up a security business and supporting a charity. We know now that having childcare, and both of us claiming back our old turf, is what works best for our family.

It would be a lie to say that I no longer have any terrible times with guilt. I do. It tends to creep up on me these days, rather than being something I live with at all times. But I do think there's a flipside to my situation, in that I dedicate quality time to my family. Work is allowed to make a fleeting appearance now and then at weekends

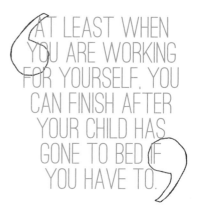

AT LEAST WHEN YOU ARE WORKING FOR YOURSELF, YOU CAN FINISH AFTER YOUR CHILD HAS GONE TO BED IF YOU HAVE TO.

because it's my hobby and I enjoy it. But I cherish my time with my son. Saturdays and Sundays are spent together and we love being in each other's company. It was a major turning point when I finally realised that even being a full-time mother wouldn't necessarily be better for us, nor that if I was working for someone else that I would have had an easier time of it. The grass isn't always greener. If I did it all again, it would be so much easier – I'd have put those demons to bed.

In any case, I had to work. I had a mortgage, bills to pay. If I wasn't running my own business, I'd have been toiling long hours for someone else. At least when you are working for yourself, you can finish after your child has gone to bed if you have to. Harry is proud of what I do – he often asks if the chair he asked me to save by my desk for him is still there. (I tell him it is, but he will need to get his exams and work hard otherwise he can't come and work in the company.) If I could go back and talk to the girl I was, fighting so hard for everything, I would say: drop the guilt. It has no place taking up your energy – use it instead to give Harry and Frank an extra long hug when you get home.

SOPHIE'S STORY

I'd always worked as a mother. I went back to my job in advertising full-time – very full-time – when Ollie was five months old. I was a master of the working-mother tricks, such as wearing a bathrobe over the business suit so the mashed Weetabix flung at you two minutes before leaving the house didn't matter. I would drop him at day-care nursery and then run for the train. It was stressful but at least the childcare was always there (except for the days when he was ill, having picked up the illness at the nursery in the first place, but then not allowed through the door with *that* cold).

Giving up work was not something I wanted to do, but I did feel a bit caught, lost in that middle ground. In the office, you're not one of the gang anymore – no more after-work cocktails, no time to gossip round the water cooler. At home, I wasn't one of the mums on a regular coffee morning. That was fine with me because I had never felt that world was my destiny, but I did miss the closeness and support I imagined they had with each other.

Being a mother was something I had always wanted in life. Even when I was planning my career according to *Girl About Town* magazine, I was planning my family, too. I wanted six children, in fact. With career and babies firmly on my agenda, I realised early on that I was going to

Me, Harry and Frank in Sydney in 2010 (left) and on a snowy day in Chiswick in 2009.

Us three in 2011 on *that* holiday. *Holly*

With Harry in Mauritius, when he was four, our first proper break.

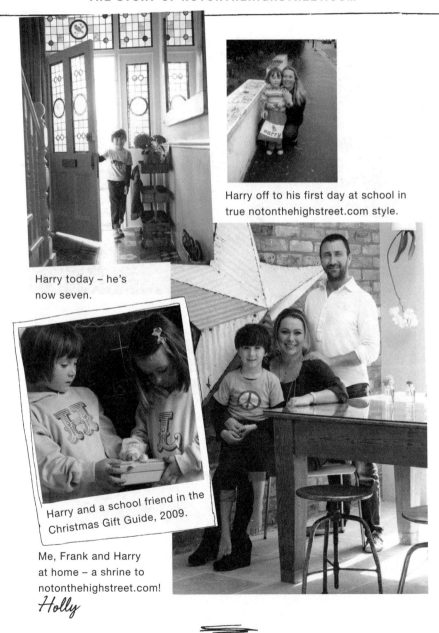

Harry off to his first day at school in true notonthehighstreet.com style.

Harry today – he's now seven.

Harry and a school friend in the Christmas Gift Guide, 2009.

Me, Frank and Harry at home – a shrine to notonthehighstreet.com!

Holly

Ollie and Honor, visiting my big sister Polly in Australia, 2003.

Honor's star appearance in the Summer Gift Guide, 2008.

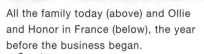

All the family today (above) and Ollie and Honor in France (below), the year before the business began.

Sophie

Me and Honor in Mauritius, 2011. The first swish holiday I could treat the family to.

With my little sisters – Claudia and me at Emily's wedding.

Simon in the kitchen – he always cooks (and Rufus thinks he's great).

Ollie, Simon and me in France, 2010. Honor broke her arm, poor thing, and hasn't been persuaded to go skiing again since.

Sophie

need to be in a good position both financially and in my career. I'd have to be highly successful, indispensable and well paid, so that I could dictate my terms and juggle all those babies around my job. I worked all this out around the age of ten. In some ways, the success I wanted was a means to an end; I felt that a better position at work would mean I could be a great mum. Even though a lovely husband and daddy for my children was part of that plan, I can safely say that it never once occurred to me that there was an easy alternative – that I could make the babies and the man could make the money.

Sophie with Honor and Ollie

However, when my second child, Honor, was born, I realised that the money wasn't stacking up and juggling two little ones under three years old was going to be a cliff-face of a challenge in the view of a three-hour round-trip commute each day in a job that was only really meant for women with zero personal commitments. Then, when I was on maternity leave, I was offered some really nice work for a magazine, so it was a case of – 'Why wouldn't you?'

When Holly approached me about going into business with her, I was living – or rather working – in a twilight zone. The children had started school and I was working part-time or on short contracts – whether a six-month stint as a features editor to cover maternity leave at IPC Media, or writing a book about weddings, or trying to start up the floristry business – which meant my childcare was always ad hoc, stretching out nursery school or primary school hours with some after-school clubs or friends or a childminder. That, in itself, is ridiculously stressful. I envied people with full-time nannies, fantasising – seething – about a life where you would just get up, make yourself look nice and leave the house when the nanny arrived.

For the first year of notonthehighstreet.com, I continued like that. School, friends, childminder, sisters and mum sometimes (though they had precious little time of their own), and even an au pair for a while. Each of which, hastily patched together into a messy whole, was unsatisfactory and debilitating. I was constantly making calls to pull in favours or apologising for being late, whether at work or to collect the children. But we couldn't afford childcare-de-luxe at that stage. Things had gone sour in the City, the culture had completely changed, so Simon was working all hours too – we couldn't chance his wage. What he earned covered the mortgage and bills, and we needed all of that. What it didn't cover was a nanny too and, as Holly and I were not yet drawing a salary, there wasn't an extra penny to go round.

It was a really strenuous time. Early drop-and-runs at miserable school breakfast clubs and then working until 1am night after night, often later, playing tag with an overstretched, overtired husband, constantly begging favours that I was never going to be able to repay. I remember some very dark days, never seeing the children. Honor wears her heart on her sleeve, so we were able to talk it out, and she knew how much I missed her. It was deeply worrying when Ollie started showing signs of damage six months in. He's a very sweet but not clingy child and one night I came in, after about four or five nights of having not seen him. He was very distraught and upset, and Simon was looking just as much so. I thought something terrible must have happened, some bad news. But no. He'd just reached a tipping point. Even a self-sufficient, confident and stable 9-year-old boy feels abandoned eventually. I had to do something – it was horrible and I was shocked at how bad I had let things get.

Finally, when we started taking a small salary – around about the time of the first investment – I was able to get a nanny. She didn't need to be full-time, but it wasn't far off. Victoria came into our lives. She was a total wonder and saint who made everything alright. The children had a brilliant few years with her – she made them pancakes for breakfast, helped them with their homework (she's half-Spanish and Ollie is still streets ahead of his peers on that one), made them lovely teas and cakes and suppers. She even made Honor's bridesmaid's dress for my sister's wedding – in fact, she altered the wedding dress when it was too big on the day itself! She propped my whole family up when my father became ill and never, ever once complained about my hideously unpredictable hours. And, when we decided that a dog was what was needed to complete our family, she trained and raised puppy Rufus to be the most obedient, loved and loving creature, complete with a whole repertoire of highly entertaining tricks.

We had some other lucky breaks, too – not least of all with the support my friends gave me when it came to the children. Not so much lifts and practical issues, though that all helps enormously, but in terms of looking out for us and making sure the children don't feel left out of anything. One friend, Amanda, always has both of them for a few days in the long holidays. She has a boy and a girl of the same age as mine and she takes them all to a show, swimming and shopping, generally letting my children know that there's another family in whose bosom they totally belong. Plus, Amanda knows it's good for me to know they're getting that with her if not me. Stephanie, my best friend, has had Honor over every Wednesday for years. Swimming lessons, tea, family life. Honor is almost the fourth child in that family and loves it. But again, that's Steph looking out for me as well as them. My family, too, have made it all so much easier and happier. My sisters have always applied themselves heartily and very lovingly to the serious responsibility of being aunties. I'm fortunate, too, that my mum understands – perhaps better than many others of her generation – the sometimes tortuous lot of a working mother, so she has come to my rescue whenever she could, as well as taking Ollie and Honor off to her house in Wales for a week every summer to give me a clear run of guilt-free, crazy-hours work time.

These days – now that Victoria has left and had her own baby, and the children are fifteen and thirteen years old – we're just getting by again. There's no such thing as childcare for teenagers, which isn't ideal if they're on their own for long stretches, but we manage. I do the mornings (kit bags, packed lunches, forgotten homework, lost school ties) and Simon does the evenings (supper, rugby training, rowing training, homework-before-it's-forgotten). We have a good balance, and Simon carries a massive share of the domestic burden. He's very good at it. His mum did me a huge favour there, raising him never to expect a woman to run around after him, and she taught him how to be a great cook, too. When he is out late with clients, as he often is, we're fortunate to have a very lovely friend and neighbour, Nicki, who bails me out and takes them in alongside her own teenage children when I realise there is no one home to feed mine or beat them into doing their homework.

And it's not all bad. I think the children appreciate what we do. Perhaps they have had to learn to fend for themselves and be independent a little too young, but they have grown up in a family where people are industrious and get rewarded for it. I think it's incredibly important as a mother to lead by example. They know about taking responsibility for their own future and already seem to have ambitions and ideals of their own, which makes me very proud. They don't seem to be damaged by

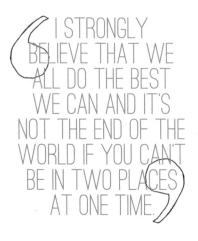

I STRONGLY BELIEVE THAT WE ALL DO THE BEST WE CAN AND IT'S NOT THE END OF THE WORLD IF YOU CAN'T BE IN TWO PLACES AT ONE TIME.

those tough years, and perhaps it did help that I was a little more at their disposal during the formative ones, standing us all in good stead and providing them with stability.

Guilt, of course, is a factor in my life as a mother. It's an almost constant thing – and perhaps as much down to my own personality as anything. I feel guilty when I think the dog doesn't like his breakfast, let alone whether or not I'm a good mother. It's something I've learned to live with. But I refuse to be made to feel guilty by other people. The sort who say, 'Gosh, I don't know how you do that. I couldn't leave my children with a stranger all day . . .' I'll admit to sadness, yes, at missing things. Not forgetting stress, pressure and sheer exhaustion at juggling things to the limit. But not guilt. It has no relevance when someone else tries to lay it at my door.

We're out there earning a living to put a roof over all their heads and hopefully provide for their future too. I don't want them to thank me for it – no child should be told you're not around much so that they 'can have nice things' – but I do think it's quite straightforward for them. It's not too difficult for a basically balanced child to work out that it's not all one big party and you can't be at their beck and call 24/7. I'm already on record as saying that I have missed parents' evenings and rugby matches, because I strongly believe that we all do the best we can and it's not the end of the world if you can't be in two places at one time. If I have to miss a school appointment, Simon can go or I'll have a meeting with the teachers another time. Or do the whole thing by email, as when Holly and I had a business trip to Silicon Valley and it coincided with Simon having to be away for work too.

We don't always get it right, but nor do non-working parents – in fact, we could learn a lot from their altogether less hung-up approach. One of my close friends is an aromatherapist and much more able to work around her children's schedules as needed, but she used to skip half of those primary school assemblies anyway. 'Eugh, they're so boring. And my girls don't want me to go anyway, to watch them perform some stupid dance they never wanted to do in the first place. We'll have much more fun going out for pizza together later,' she told me once. This isn't neglect – this is getting your priorities right. There's a pressure on today's working mothers to right the wrongs of every failed parent everywhere and it's all so much nonsense.

Perhaps I would have done it differently, but I don't know how. Holly and I just did what we had to do. We were in it so deep and had so much to lose from such an early stage that we genuinely felt we had no choice. So we just got on with it. If you get your business right, your home life will start to make sense and the tough times you have all been through will be worth it. It was for us – we sincerely hope it is for you, too.

AFTERWORD

WOMEN MEAN BUSINESS

'No one should have to dance
backward all their lives.'

Jill Ruckelhaus

This is an afterword – not an afterthought. Having
reached the end of the book and demonstrated how almost anybody can
set up and run their own business – not just women – it should be clear
that we are not whingers. We had an idea, and we ran with it and made
it happen. The fact that we are female was by the by. That said, we
encountered some patronising attitudes along the way, and as 90 per cent
of our partners are women and 95 per cent of our customers are of the
same fair sex, we do feel compelled to say something on all our behalfs.

We want to stand up for all the right things – success, equality, the
removal of barriers, opportunity and culture change. But there's a crucial
point that no one seems to be making at the moment: the argument has
to be relevant, interesting and include the balance of male and female
synergies to have merit.

We need to kick out the misplaced notion that if you keep putting
businesswomen in a room together, something will change. It changes by
getting out there and doing something, not by sitting on a panel without
a man in sight, ranting on about exclusively female issues. We need to

redefine the cause or it will be something successful women distance themselves from.

Holly: 'I was recently invited to talk on an all-female panel. That in itself felt old-fashioned. Why not hear men's experience in growing business with women? But it was when I was asked, "How does being a female entrepreneur make you better than your male counterparts?" that I realised I had made a wasted journey. We should all have moved on from debating those sorts of questions by now.'

Because work still needs to be done. The average annual wage for a man in the UK is £30,817. For a woman, £24,069. Over a working lifetime of, say, forty years, that can add up to a difference of almost £270,000. That could mean the difference between an old age in poverty and an old age in comfort. Not to mention that women rarely get to work the full forty years, once you add in maternity leave, years taken out of paid employment to raise a family, and the fact that it is usually women who become the chief carers of elderly parents or close family with special needs. In other words, for all the noise that is being made, statistically it's not working.

Running your own business does mean that you get to take charge of your own life to a much greater degree. You can pay yourself and your staff fair wages. There is no glass ceiling. For women who are trying to work from home in order to have better flexibility with their hours around their family's needs, managing their own company can provide a lot of the answers. But not all of them.

Let's be clear about one thing – we like men. We see no reason to dislike them as a species any more than we love every single woman we meet. But there's no doubt that a few of the males we have come across have projected onto us their own stereotyped ideas of working women. The most infuriating phrase for us to hear is when a man says of a woman he knows, 'She didn't want to go back to work, so she started her own business.' It's not about not working, doofus, it's about working differently. We need collectively to put to one side the notion that starting up your own business is a shirker's option – if you're a woman. As the rest of this book should have made clear, that is patently not the case.

What's more, while many women choose to start their own business in an area in which they feel particularly comfortable – the domestic, retail, fashion, baby and children's markets – that doesn't mean that they are not completely serious about conquering those markets. A woman who tells you that she is setting up a company that sells, say, kitchen equipment should not be patronised as indulging in a passion for cooking. (She may have a passion for cooking – that's what will make her good at the business. But she will also have a passion for making money.)

Nor should a woman who goes into any of the more 'male' markets – accountancy, finance, manufacturing, sport – be seen as a woman making it in a man's world and having to do it all on their terms. Karren Brady, now the Vice Chairman of West Ham United at the age of forty-three, became the youngest managing director of a public company when Birmingham City Football Club floated on the London Stock Exchange in 1997. She did not see that she needed to cut her hair short or dress more like a man in order to win the respect she needed in the boardroom. She did it by being good at her job.

Nevertheless, there are cultural issues around being a woman in the workplace, not least when it comes to money. We all know that women are generally poor at asking for a due pay rise or negotiating a better starting salary (male graduates tend to have better starting salaries than female graduates – this is due not so much to companies offering women employees less money, but because men often refuse the first offer and only accept a raised one). But what is less talked about is that women have been largely under-educated when it comes to the whys and where-fores of how money works, and this puts them on the back foot when it comes to raising investment.

When you start a business, money is tight at the beginning and is usually tight for quite some time. Of those we asked, the majority of our partners did not begin to pay themselves until they had been up and running for at least two years. That's a lot of mortgage payments and bills to cover with no wages in sight. Many of those businesses funded themselves through credit cards rather than investment. Start-up grants barely exist and are so much trouble to apply for that it is hard to justify the time spent on the forms for the return they bring.

Sophie: 'It took me until my third business to find out what venture capital and angel investment really were. Shamefully, before that point, I thought they were rather otherworldly things. They were terms bandied about by men who also talked about bear markets and bull markets – and I wasn't completely sure what they were either. Nor am I alone. Women-led companies receive less than 10 per cent of all investment.'

Why are women doing so badly when it comes to investment? We have a hunch it's because many venture capitalists and business angels assume only a single or wife-at-home man can give them the commitment they need. (Luckily, ours were rather more savvy.) But this needs to be changed, because for women with big – that is, expensive – ambitions, VCs and angels make sense. Learning to walk the walk and talk the talk, as we explain in Chapter 6, is not only vital to your understanding of your business, it will also contribute to the wider need for this culture change.

There's another huge concern when it comes to women and money: childcare costs.

A recent report showed that childcare is the elephant in the room when it comes to discussing why more women aren't in the top positions at work. Not so much for those at board level – by that point either they can afford childcare, or they're at an age where their children no longer need it – but earlier on, when it comes to encouraging women back to work after they've had their babies. Women who don't get back onto the career ladder halfway up have no hope of climbing to the top.

Until childcare is tax deductible, we do not believe that the playing field is level for mothers who are starting up businesses. Working tax credits, while laudable, only apply to those on a very low income. Women who earn above average wages – often those who are creating further employment and boosting the UK economy – tend also to choose above average childcare costs, whether for a full-time nanny or nursery. It is not unusual for a third of a woman's *gross* income to be spent on childcare, after she has paid income tax. Nor is this particular to high earners. Many women choose to return to work part-time after having their children, simply so as to stay in the marketplace for their career. Women are better educated now and, as they are having their children later, their careers are better established. But no one is irreplaceable, and it is too risky to take five years off and hope to get the same job again. In the twenty-first century, with technology changing at a fast and constant pace, it is even easier to get left behind. Taking a wage that leaves almost nothing to spare after childcare and tax have been paid is a compromise many are forced to make so as not to lose their career foothold. With so little to spare in their purses, these women are not going to be boosting consumer spend or reinvesting into the national economy.

We're proud to say that our partners are making a positive effort to make it better for women. Betsy Benn, founder of her own eponymous business creating personalised prints, took redundancy from a corporate job when she started a family because she wanted to spend time with her baby and because, as she says, 'Childcare costs were just daft anyway.' Two years later, her company employs between two and six people, depending on the time of year and seasonal peaks, actively recruiting others that were in her position – a mum wanting to get back to work – and offering them an exciting opportunity. But unless those women can make the childcare/salary equation work in their favour, they can't take that life-changing chance.

Until there are proper tax breaks available on childcare, women's potential earning power and national economic contribution is being stunted by the government.

Holly: 'When we were starting the business, having full-time childcare meant the difference between success and failure. But we couldn't afford it. We would have had to earn – as any woman does – around £40,000 a year just to break even. Forty thousand pounds a year will pay the income tax bill and a full-time nanny, that's all. It won't pay the mortgage or rent, food bills, clothing, heating, phone . . . That's shocking. Yet our business was not only pumping huge sums of money into the economy – approaching £100 million – it was enabling other businesses to grow. Of course, many of those small company owners suffered the same childcare difficulties that we did. There is no solution yet, no real proposal from the government to tackle it. That is very, very wrong.'

Nor should the childcare issue be exclusively a mother's concern. The parenting landscape is changing rapidly, too. In Gaby Hinsliff's book *Half a Wife* (Chatto & Windus, 2012), she writes about how fathers are increasing their time with their families – by 2003, men were doing around a quarter of the family's child-related tasks during the week and a third of them on weekends. In couples where both work full-time, the men were doing slightly more than that. Furthermore, men want to share in the

WE HOPE WE HAVE SHOWN YOU THAT THERE IS A WAY TO ACHIEVE A GREAT WORKING LIFE FOR WOMEN ON THEIR OWN GOOD TERMS.

childcare. Hinsliff quotes compelling statistics that show that eight in ten Britons think that ideally men and women should share responsibility for raising their children, and 72 per cent think they should share responsibility for bringing in the household income.

We know that we can only make our lives function properly if we have true equality at work and at home. When our husbands or partners cook supper one night or put on a washing load without being asked, they are not being 'marvellously helpful' as our mothers might say, they are working as part of the team. Equally, we have to be prepared to shoulder half of the worry and effort to bring in the money. If the woman is the one earning more money, she doesn't expect to be praised in public by her husband for being extra helpful and nice. It's simply her half of what she brings to the table.

We are getting there. We know we are because we can see the changes happening all around us, with our friends and the partners who sell through the business. All our daughters, we believe, will be having very different conversations with their future husbands when it comes to making decisions about how the household will be run and how the children will be looked after.

We would like to think that we have shown you that there is a way to achieve a great working life for women on their own good terms. If you act with confidence and do a competent job, then you deserve to be rewarded on your merit. And if you can work to achieve a wider cultural change for the better, by educating your sons as well as your daughters on the benefits of teamwork when it comes to running a household and raising a family, then you should sleep well at night, too.

Sweet dreams. We hope they come true for you.

Holly Sophie

JARGON BUSTER

Above-the-line advertising: Advertising typically directed at a large audience through mass media channels such as newspaper or magazine print, television, or radio. Below-the-line advertising, on the other hand, refers to more direct forms of marketing such as direct mail or promotional events.

Affiliate marketing: When another website displays a link or banner advertising your own website. You can pay for this service (through a pay-per-click scheme, or in commission on resulting sales) or come to a mutually beneficial agreement with third-party sites (maybe you carry a link to their website in return). See Chapter 5 for more.

Audience: Another word for potential customers and, in marketing, the people or segment at whom your marketing message is aimed. For example, the online users of a site you feature on, or visitors at a sponsored event.

Banner: A web or display banner is an online advertisement space sold under an affiliate marketing agreement, through a direct deal with the advertiser, or via a banner ad network. Usually short and wide or tall and thin in appearance, banners promote traffic to your website from third-party sites through a clickable design. See Chapter 5 for more.

Balance sheet: A statement of the business' assets (machinery, cash, stock and so on) and its liabilities (what you owe to suppliers, HMRC and others) at that point in time.

Blog: A website publishing experiences, opinions and/or observations – akin to an online journal – and an increasingly popular channel for business as well as personal use. Blogs are usually owned and contributed to by one person, or in some cases a small group, with readers able to interact and comment on 'posts' – whether text, images, or both – left by the author. See Chapter 5 for more.

Bottom line: The net (or overall) profit or loss of a business.

Bottom-up pricing: A means of calculating the best price point for your product(s), based first and foremost on any production costs. You will also need to look at sales-based and top-down pricing. See Chapter 6 for more.

Brochure site: A website with pages of non-interactive content, for example an online version of a catalogue for browsing.

Business angel: A wealthy individual who uses his or her own money to invest in a business in return for equity. See Chapter 6 for more.

Call to action: A term to describe the direction given to consumers by a piece of advertising or marketing material; for example, 'Click here to redeem your voucher' or 'Visit www.notonthehighstreet.com for more information'.

Capital depreciation: A calculation of the amount by which any capital assets lose value over time, an important consideration when drawing up your P&L forecast. See Chapter 6 for more.

Capital costs: The amount of money spent on equipment or machinery (otherwise known as capital assets) needed for your business. In accounting, you might hear capital costs referred to as 'fixed assets'.

Cash flow forecast: A spreadsheet showing your business income (money coming in) and expenses (money paid out) over a certain amount of time (usually a minimum of twenty-four months). The cash flow forecast is an integral part of your business plan. See Chapter 6 for more.

CFO: Chief financial officer.

Copyright: An exclusive legal right that arises automatically upon creation of a literary, artistic or creative work, protecting that work from copy (and, to certain extents, use) by anyone other than the person who wrote, made or designed it. See Chapter 2 for more.

Core offering: The primary benefit offered to consumers by your product or service.

Corporation tax: Tax paid to HMRC on the profits of a limited company, at 24 per cent at the time of writing (though lower rates apply for small businesses with taxable profits below a certain threshold). Visit the HMRC website for more information.

Creditor: Any person or business to whom you owe money.

Direct mail: Any piece of marketing material sent directly to consumers, for example an addressed catalogue or a promotional letter to existing customers. See Chapter 5 for more.

Distance Selling Regulations (DSRs): UK legislation designed to protect consumers not physically present at the time they make a purchase from a business. The legislation therefore applies to all consumer trans-actions made over the phone, online, by email or by mail order. Visit Business Link for more information.

Distribution list: A group of email contacts, meaning you can quickly and easily send a piece of mail to multiple addresses at once. Distribution lists are commonly offered by email programs and providers such as Microsoft Outlook or Google Mail, and are useful if you need to send a targeted message to contacts that fall within a particular category without inserting each address individually (for example a press release to all national news desks).

Display advertising: A means of online marketing whereby advertisements to third-party websites appear online in display banners. See Chapter 5 for more.

Disposable income: The amount of spending or saving money available to a consumer or household once their taxes have been deducted from their income.

Dividends: An amount paid out to shareholders of a company from after-tax profits.

Domain name: See URL.

Door drop: Any piece of unaddressed marketing material delivered to consumers, for example a company brochure or take-away menu.

Due diligence: A detailed review of company information that usually takes place before an agreement or sale. The bigger the agreement, the more comprehensive the investigation; venture capitalists, for example, will require an in-depth audit of financial accounts and company history, as well as a personal background check, before signing on the dotted line.

E-commerce: The buying or selling of products by electronic means – most commonly online, but email and fax transactions count too.

Economies of scale: The amount of money a business can save when expanding its operations. For example, the cost-per-unit tends to drop when buying mass-produced items in large quantities, and lower rates of interest are often available to big companies able to borrow large amounts of money.

Email marketing: A marketing channel in which specific consumers are targeted by email. See Chapter 5 for more.

Embargo: A PR term requesting that the recipient of a piece of material does not publish it until a specified date. If you are launching a product or service, or want to release some important information on a certain date, sending the information in an advance press release with an 'Embargoed until' date allows journalists to prepare their story in time to coincide with your announcement, with an understanding that your message must not be leaked before that date. A press embargo is not legally binding, but journalists honour such requests so as to maintain good relationships with sources of news-worthy information.

Elevator pitch: A phrase coined to describe the few sentences that capture your business. It's the pitch a business owner would make if they found themselves sharing a lift with the perfect investor and had just a few seconds to get their message across.

Equity: The ownership interest of investors in a company, i.e. the stake in that company they are entitled to in return for their money.

Equity finance: Selling shares in a company as a means of raising money.

Exit: When an investor sells his or her stake in a company, taking any profits or losses relative to their share.

Financial forecast: A calculated prediction of a company's finances over a certain period of time. Drawing up a cash flow forecast and P&L forecast are essential when starting a business, and should be repeated frequently after that. See Chapter 6 for more.

Fixed costs: Costs necessary in providing a product or service that are not dependent on how many are sold. For example, the cost of renting a premises or monthly internet fees.

Gross: The entire sum of what you get paid, before any taxes (for example VAT) are paid out.

Hidden costs: Costs that you might not initially think of first time around. When buying a computer, for example, is there any software that you will need to upgrade down the line? Is your sewing machine going to need a regular service to maintain its use? Are you still using the home printer, when you ought to buy a new one?

Hi-res/low-res image: Image resolution describes the detail an image holds, so the higher the number, the more detail the image has and the better the quality. Hi-res is what you need for printing a full-page image on a website, but you only need low-res if you are emailing a picture as a reference (not for printing).

Hosting service: A company that effectively sells space on the web, allowing you to pick a domain name and use their hosting servers to hold your website.

Hyperlink: A clickable image or piece of text that directs the user somewhere else, either to another page within the same site or to another website. For example, the text, images and URLs that appear in search engine results that take you to the chosen page.

Intellectual property (IP): This is a catch-all phrase that includes the non-physical elements of your business that need legal protection. Intellectual property law is made up of many elements of intellectual property rights (IPRs) including: trademarks, copyright, patents and registered design and unregistered design rights. See Chapter 2 for more.

Investors: Bodies or individuals (such as business angels and venture capitalists) who put money into a business in return for a share of owner-ship, or equity. See Chapter 6 for more.

Key performance indicators (KPIs): The term used to describe factors used in measuring the most important indicators of company performance over an amount of time. KPIs will range from business to business (and department to department), but common examples might include the number of new customers acquired, the percentage of customer service enquiries resolved positively, or simply the amount of turnover generated by a particular activity.

Keywords: A marketing term used to describe one or more word commonly used by consumers when searching for a particular product or service. Defining and measuring these words is particularly important for SEO purposes.

Lead: A potential customer.

Limited company: A company owned entirely by its shareholders, with limited financial liability. There are two types of limited company: public and private. Business Link and Companies House can help you find out what the right type of business is for you.

NDA: Non-disclosure agreement – a legally binding contract signed by all parties agreeing to confidentiality, either between private individuals or whole companies.

Net profit: The money left over after all costs and taxes are paid.

Open rate: A term to describe the percentage of recipients who open a piece of email marketing material, as opposed to those who delete without reading.

Organic/natural results: When you type a word or phrase into a search engine, these are the results that appear on the list purely because of their relevance to your enquiry, as opposed to paid search results.

Overhead costs: Ongoing costs necessary to running a business, for example rent and utilities, insurance or accountancy fees.

Paid results: In marketing, exactly what it says on the tin. Unlike organic/natural results, these appear in premium spots on the search engine results page (usually at the top, or to one side) as a result of PPC advertising. See Chapter 5 for more.

Patent: A form of intellectual property that protects new inventions, their function and the way that they work to achieve it. Filing for a patent can be complex and expensive, and an invention needs to fulfil certain criteria before it can be protected. The Intellectual Property Office can tell you more.

Pay-per-click (PPC): A marketing technique used to promote search results, encouraging traffic to sponsored sites. Each time a user clicks on a paid result, the owner of the promoted website is charged a pre-defined amount. See Chapter 5 for more.

PR: Or public relations, as it is now less commonly known. PR falls under the umbrella of marketing, and essentially functions to maintain the public image of a company or person. See Chapters 4 and 5 for more.

Press advertising: Advertisement space sold in newspapers or magazines, in a range of sizes. You can often buy print and online space together within the same publication. See Chapter 5 for more.

Price point: Quite simply the price of a product or service. You will initially need to determine how much you will sell for by using the bottom-up, top-down or sales-based pricing methods. See Chapter 6 for more.

Primary research: A means of gathering information directly from consumers, either by observation or interview. For example, by conducting a survey on your local high street or sending an email questionnaire. Primary research can be time-consuming and you might find that many people say they are too busy to take part but it can be a good way of getting in-depth answers that are directly relevant to your business.

Profit and loss forecast (P&L): A spreadsheet showing the revenue and service outgoings over a given period (usually twenty-four months), indicating whether and at which point your business will make or lose money. See Chapter 6 for more.

Profit margin: Refers to the money you make after your costs have been paid for. You can increase your profit margin by reducing costs or increasing the price of the product/service sold and vice versa.

Projection: see financial forecast. Also may be a forecast of other data, such as number of customers.

Raw materials: Any unfinished substance or material used in making a product to its finished state. For example, a piece of silk thread used to hand-embroider a cushion, or a pot of ink used to make a letterpress print.

Reach: A term used to denote the extent or application of a message to customers.

Retargeting: A means of directing a display banner advertisement to targeted customers, normally to incentivise those who have viewed a product online but decided not to purchase. See Chapter 5 for more.

Revenue: Any money that comes in to the business as a result of normal business activities, meaning revenue is usually derived from selling goods or services. Also known as turnover.

Risk capital: A sum of money invested in a business that is at risk of not being repaid. This may be the case with loans granted by friends and family.

Route to market: In a nutshell: how, where and when you sell your product or service. See Chapter 3 for more.

Run rate (finance): How a company's future performance might look if based on recent achievements. For example, the number of sales predicted for the coming year based solely on those made over the last quarter.

Sales volumes: The quantity of products or services sold over an amount of time.

Sales-based pricing: A factor in determining the price point of your product, taking your annual sales target as a starting point. This should be used in conjunction with bottom-up and top-down pricing methods. See Chapter 6 for more.

Scaling up: As your business revenue grows, you will inevitably need to expand proportionally. This could mean renting larger premises, taking on employees, upgrading tools and equipment, working longer hours and so on.

Search engine optimisation (SEO): A means of marketing your business with the specific aim of it appearing high in the organic/natural results lists of an online search engine. See Chapter 5 for more.

Secured loan: A loan provided by a bank or other lender that is secured against an asset belonging to you or your business. The most common example is a mortgage against property; should you default on repayments, your creditor is liable to take that property and retrieve the value they are owed. See Chapter 6 for more.

Shareholder/stakeholder: Any person or organisation that owns at least one share, or equity, in a company.

Shareholding/stakeholding: The percentage or proportion of equity owned by a person or organisation relative to the total number of shares within a company.

Social media: The most engaging marketing tools of our time, social media channels such as Twitter, Facebook, Google+ and Pinterest are changing the way businesses promote their products and services, and interact with their customers. See Chapter 5 for more.

Sole trader: The simplest way to run a business, setting up as a sole trader does not require registering a company with Companies House. You must, however, register as self-employed with HMRC. Keeping records and accounts is straightforward, and you get to keep all the profits. However, sole traders are personally liable for any debts that their business runs up, making this a risky option for businesses that require a lot of investment. Business Link and Companies House can help you find out what the right type of business is for you.

Subscriber list: A database of the email and/or postal addresses of people who receive information about your company. It's important to comply with the Data Protection Act when holding such data – visit the Information Commissioner's Office (ICO) website to learn more.

Target demographic: A group of people to whom a company targets its product or service, and logically its marketing and advertising efforts too. Demographics include age, gender, income, health, education, nationality and so on.

Tax deductible: A term describing any costs that can be used to reduce your taxable income and end-of-year tax bill, in most cases because the expense was necessary to the function of your business. The Business Link and HMRC websites can tell you more.

Thumbnails: Reduced-size images that usually accompany a larger image. Thumbnails allow the consumer to view multiple images at once – for example of various aspects or colours of a product – and often, when clicked, enable the consumer to view a bigger, hi-res version of the selected picture through hyperlink.

Top-down pricing: To be used in conjunction with bottom-up and sales-based pricing methods, top-down pricing is a means of ascertaining a suitable price point for a product or service against what consumers would be willing to pay. See Chapter 6 for more.

Top line (finance): Sales or revenue.

Trademark: Your brand's distinguishing mark, represented by a graphically designed sign or badge. Customers are thus able to identify you and your products quickly. A trademark can be: a logo or symbol (the Nike tick); a company name (ACME Ltd); a brand name (Virgin); a sign or shape (the bottle owned by Coca-Cola); a colour (Pantone 151 owned by Orange Brand Services Ltd); or a word, phrase or slogan ('Stella Artois . . . reassuringly expensive'). See Chapter 2 for more.

Traffic: The number of people that use a website, measured in terms of visitors and page views. The number of visitors to a site will invariably be lower than the number of page views, since only one site visit will be counted regardless of the number of pages that visitor clicks through to. Traffic can be an important KPI and is useful in monitoring how a customer uses your website and for how long.

Transactional site: A website on which users can either buy products or book services. See Chapter 4 for more.

Turnover: The total value of sales over a certain period. Also known as revenue.

Unsecured loan: Money borrowed from a bank or other lender that, unlike a secured loan, does not give the creditor any rights over the borrower's assets. This increased risk means interest on unsecured loans is usually higher than on secured loans. See Chapter 6 for more.

URL: A 'uniform resource locator', otherwise known as the global address of a website – for example www.notonthehighstreet.com.

USP: The unique selling proposition of your product or service that makes it stand out from its competitors.

Value added tax (VAT): A percentage of your sales price (currently at 20 per cent) which you charge your customer, and then pass along to the government, less VAT you have incurred on your costs (see tax deductible). Only businesses with a turnover of more than a certain amount need to be registered for VAT (see VAT threshold). See Chapter 6 and the HMRC website for more.

Variable costs: Any expense associated with producing your product or service that changes according to the quantity you sell (unlike fixed costs). For example, raw materials, delivery costs or labour.

VAT threshold: The amount of turnover a company can achieve before needing to register for VAT with HMRC, currently at £77,000. This figure changes annually and businesses have to take the responsibility of checking it.

Venture capital: Money invested in a business by a professional investment company (venture capitalists) in return for equity in that business. See Chapter 6 for more.

THE DIRECTORY

REGISTRATIONS AND REGULATIONS

Resources

Companies House..companieshouse.gov.uk

Companies House WebCheck service wck2.companieshouse.gov.uk

Data Protection Act – a guide to ....ico.gov.uk

Directgov – Official UK Government..direct.gov.uk

Distance Selling Regulations – a guide to ....oft.gov.uk/ds-explained

HM Revenue & Customs (HMRC) ....hmrc.gov.uk

RESEARCH AND SUPPORT

Resources

British Library Business & IP Centre..bl.uk/bipc

Business Link – Support, information and advice..................businesslink.gov.uk

HMRC Business Education and Support ....hmrc.gov.uk/bst

Office for National Statistics ....ons.gov.uk

SmallBusiness Advice UK..smallbusiness.co.uk

Tools

RationalSurvey .... rationalsurvey.com

Smart-Survey .... smart-survey.co.uk

SurveyMonkey .... surveymonkey.com

LEGAL ADVICE

Resources

Anti Copying in Design .... acid.eu.com

Chartered Society of Designers .... csd.org.uk

Copyright Licensing Agency .... cla.co.uk

Design and Artists Copyright Society .... dacs.org.uk

European Trademarks and Designs Registry .... oami.europa.eu

The Federation of Small Businesses .... fsb.org.uk

Institute of Trademark Attorneys .... itma.org.uk

International Property Office .... ipo.gov.uk

The Law Society .... lawsociety.org.uk

OWN IT .... own-it.org

MARKETING

Affiliate marketing

Affiliate Window .... affiliatewindow.com

Commission Junction .... uk.cj.com

LinkShare .... linkshare.com

TradeDoubler .... tradedoubler.com

Webgains .... webgains.com

Display advertising

Criteo .... criteo.com

Google Adsense .... google.co.uk/adsense

Google Display Network .... google.co.uk/adwords/displaynetwork

Struq .... struq.com

Email marketing

Campaign Monitor .... campaignmonitor.com

Emailvision .... emailvision.co.uk

Performance tracking

Alexa .... alexa.com

Google Analytics .... google.com/analytics

Picture editing

Adobe Photoshop .... photoshop.com

GIMP .... gimp.org

Picasa .... picasa.google.co.uk

Search engines and SEO

Bing .... bing.com

Google .... google.co.uk

Google Adwords .... google.adwords.co.uk

Microsoft adCenter .... adCenter.microsoft.com

Yahoo! .... uk.yahoo.com

Social networking, blogging and videos

AddThis..addthis.com

Facebook ....facebook.com

Google Blogspot...googleblog.blogspot.com

LinkedIn...linkedin.com

LikeMinds...wearelikeminds.com

Pinterest ....pinterest.com

TED ....ted.com

Tumblr...tumblr.com

Twitter..twitter.com

TweetStats...tweetstats.com

TweetEffect...tweeteffect.com

Wordpress..wordpress.com

Wordpress (advanced) ....wordpress.org

YouTube ....youtube.com

Online payment processing providers

PayPal...paypal.co.uk

Shopify ....shopify.com

WorldPay ....worldpay.com

OTHER USEFUL

At the office

IKEA ....ikea.co.uk

People Per Hour ....peopleperhour.com

Royal Mail...royalmail.com

Community and support

Business Plus Baby .... businessplusbaby.com

everywoman .... everywoman.com

Mum's The Boss .... mumstheboss.co.uk

Finance

ASC Finance for Business .... asc.co.uk

Experian UK .... experian.co.uk

Sage .... sage.co.uk

If you believe you have what it takes to sell with us
as a partner, please visit us to find out more at
www.notonthehighstreet.com/buildabusiness

ACKNOWLEDGEMENTS

And we thought running a company was complicated.
Our book has been in the making for as long as notonthehighstreet.com itself, and we cannot begin to thank adequately all those who have made both of those things possible. But we'll have a go.

It has been such a pleasure to work with Jessica Fellowes in writing this book. We have learned so much, and made a new and lovely friend too. Her talent as a writer is great, but her skills were so many more in making this project such an enjoyable and fruitful one. Thanks to Jessica's family, too – Simon, Beatrix, Louis and George – who have all been supportive in their different ways.

Our agent Rowan Lawton, and the team at Simon & Schuster, especially Carly Cook, instantly recognised – and then shaped – the opportunity to publish a different kind of business book. Dawn Burnett and Ally Glynn make a formidable marketing team, and we have Emma Harrow to thank for her publicity prowess, as well as others at Simon & Schuster for making this a success: Kerr MacRae, Jo Whitford, Dom Brendon, James Horobin and Jon Stefani. Our thanks to Nick Venables, who designed at lightning speed, and to our own Kate Wright and Lydia Ripper, who brought their unique style very beautifully to the book, just as they have always done to our brand.

We couldn't have produced this book without the superior knowledge and wisdom of Gail Caulfield, Jenny Hyde, Rebecca Rogers, Jim Warren and Sarah Wilson. We owe them a special note of gratitude for making us sound cleverer than we are in all the right places. Any mistakes, of course, are our own.

Without the business there would have been no book. And without the talent, commitment and sheer goodness of a few special people – Tom Teichman, Kiko Duffy, Joe Simms, Gregory Becker, Carrie Tucker, Julie Turner – there would have been no business. Mark Esiri has provided endless wisdom and support, and more recent investors Ben Holmes and Laurel Bowden have played a vital part. Lucy Wood, Summerly Devito and Emma Wood have been with us as some of the original Not Girls from the beginning, hard-working and loyal through those toughest early days. And we are so grateful to Kate Lynas and Cora Wallet, who have been our right-hand women, professional and calm, for many a challenging year. As we've grown, every single person in our enterprising and talented team – now that there are more than 100 of us, too many to list, though we are sorely tempted to try – is trusted and dear to us. We just hope they know how much we appreciate each one. In the same way, those thousands of businesses who work with us as partners of notonthehighstreet.com are a constant inspiration and a privilege to work with, whether they're the ones who have been with us since we were little more than an idea, or the newest to join the fold. Our friends Caroline Thorogood and Graham Pugh first helped us to tease out the personality of the brand, especially one fateful evening over supper; Kevin McSpadden has been an important and clever ally; and there are also many – like our first office manager Carol, our printer Nick, cabbie Lee, technical support guy Charlie, and phone man Peter – who were generous and patient when the chips were down, so we're grateful to be able to thank them now.

Which brings us to the beginning of the story, where without us there would be no business. And without our friends and families, there would definitely be no us. No sane us, anyway.

So we each want to thank our parents, who (perhaps not deliberately) raised us to be insanely driven and industrious as well as (more intentionally) to believe in ourselves and dreams, and did so much at a practical level to make sure those dreams came true. Sally and Robert Tucker, Holly's parents, bring their hard work, talent and a crucial steadying hand to the business every single day. Penny Vincenzi, Sophie's mother, has always made success look so easy and therefore worth a try, and a special thank you to Sophie's father, Paul Vincenzi, whose brave inventiveness is no longer with us.

Much of our sanity is down to our endlessly forgiving, propping and cheering sisters and friends. Holly's sister Carrie Tucker and friends Josephine Charlton, Summerly Devito, Kelly Hart, Kirstie King and Amie Pardanyi. Sophie's sisters Polly Harding, Emily Gunnis and Claudia Vincenzi and friends Stephanie Hopping, Nicki Marsh, Debbie Campbell, Amanda Erritt, Amanda Free, Elaine Gallagher and Shona Hughes. Everyone starting a business should have friends and sisters like these.

And finally, we are on our knees with gratitude to Frank and Harry, and to Simon, Ollie and Honor. Just when you thought the business was going to let up for a minute, we went and did a book. Quite how your patience and love holds out at times like these, we may never know. But we couldn't have done any of it without you.

INDEX